PLANET EARTH'S LAST HOPE

By the same author

GOD'S TRUTH—*A scientist shows why it makes sense to believe the Bible.*

ALAN HAYWARD

Planet Earth's last hope

The Christian answer to the environmental crisis

Lakeland

LAKELAND
MARSHALL, MORGAN & SCOTT
116 Baker Street
London, W1M 2BB

First published 1973
First paperback edition (revised) 1975

ISBN 0 551 00569 6

Printed in Great Britain by Cox & Wyman Ltd,
London, Reading and Fakenham

CONTENTS

ACKNOWLEDGEMENTS

Like most of my writings, this book is a result of teamwork. Numerous friends have helped me in one way or another, especially Peter Forbes, David Godfrey and Harry Whittaker who read the first draft of the first edition and suggested lots of improvements, and Rita Dyson who typed both drafts with her usual cheerful efficiency.

The second edition owes much to a correspondent, Mr. S. M. Houghton, who took the trouble to bring to my notice some inaccuracies that his eagle eye spotted in the first edition.

A.H.

PROLOGUE

A gleaming spaceship wings its silent way among the stars.

From a great distance it is a magnificent sight. It has the clean lines, the functional beauty, of a superbly designed machine.

A close-up view gives a very different impression. Blemishes appear that could not be seen from afar. The spacecraft has evidently travelled a great distance, and she has taken a battering on the voyage. Scars and patches of filth mar the shining perfection of her walls.

Aboard the mighty vessel there is an atmosphere of tension. This is very far from being a happy ship. On every hand are signs that all is not well.

Some of the basic life-support systems are evidently working inefficiently. The air is foul and the water, though drinkable, is tainted. Food and fuel are beginning to run short.

The crew's morale is in a pathetic state. Lack of leadership has proved disastrous. It is a long time now since the Captain was taken off, in answer to an urgent call to return to base.

Things have been going wrong ever since. The crew have tried to deal with the emergencies that arose, but many of the problems have been beyond their power to solve.

Now they are almost despairing of saving the ship. Each man is beginning to think of himself. Long ago they ceased to work together as one team. Instead, they have banded together in groups, with the stronger factions taking more than their fair share of the available supplies, and the weaker suffering hardship as a result.

Worst of all, they cannot agree upon what to do with their vessel. Some of them are farsighted enough to be deeply disturbed. They are painfully aware that the present course will lead to the ultimate tragedy. Unless they take some remedial action their bones will travel the infinity of space forever—a grim memorial to their own helplessness.

But these stern-faced realists trying frantically to work out a solution are in a minority. There are many cheerful optimists insisting that there is no need for alarm. They cannot, will not, dare not face the ugly facts.

Others are convinced that nothing can be done to save the situation. Their only concern is to spend their remaining days as happily as possible, before it is all over.

Meanwhile the end is drawing ever nearer. The end of a journey that began so joyously, with such high hopes and aspirations. The end of all their good intentions. The end of everything, merciless, irresistible and black.

The date is nineteen hundred and seventy five.

The name of the spaceship is The Planet Earth.[1]

I

THE MESS WE'VE MADE

I had my first real taste of air pollution in December 1952.

At the time I was living in a London suburb. One evening I had to conduct a Bible class in a meeting hall about two miles away from home. An unusually thick fog had come down during the day, so I left the car in the garage and fetched out my old bike.

By looking straight down past the front wheel I could just manage to see the kerb. It was a slow ride and an eerie one because no other traffic seemed to be about, but I got there safely in the end.

Not another soul turned up, so after waiting a while I set out for home. Then the fun really started. By this time the fog was so thick that cycling was out of the question, and the air smelt like the inside of a kipper-smoking plant.

Somehow I managed to grope my way home, where a worried wife was awaiting me.

"Sorry I'm late, darling," I apologised. "But this is no ordinary fog."

Just how extraordinary it was, neither of us had any idea at the time. It went on for five ghastly days. During that time the poisonous air killed four thousand Londoners—a far greater number than have died in any British peacetime disaster within living memory.

It was all caused by a combination of unusual weather conditions and the emissions from London's chimneys. The air high above a big city is nearly always colder than the air at ground level. This enables the warm, polluted air from the city to rise, while fresh air from elsewhere is sucked in to take its place.

On this occasion an upper layer of relatively warm, still air blanketed London, and the fumes from the capital's chimneys were unable to get away. London choked in its own smoke until at last the weather changed.

Poison Everywhere

The English air is cleaner nowadays. One experience like that was enough for the British Government. They soon passed laws limiting the emission of smoke from chimneys.

In many other countries, however, the situation has grown steadily worse. The chief offender nowadays is the internal combustion engine. Many cities are paying a fearful price for their road transport systems.

Pity the poor traffic policeman in Tokyo. After a few hours on duty he has to return to the station, there to inhale pure oxygen for a while until his lungs recover from the strain.

Civilians are catered for in Tokyo, too. Big stores are supplied with penny-in-the-slot oxygen machines, to revive choking shoppers.

At present about three tons of dirt fall each day upon every square mile of the Japanese capital. The Director of Tokyo's Pollution Research Centre predicts that there will be no improvement. On the contrary he expects the position to get rapidly worse, until in a few years' time every inhabitant has to carry a gas mask.

In some American cities the situation is not much better. A ton and a half of airborne dirt falls on each square mile of New York in a typical day. Los Angeles schoolchildren are often kept indoors at playtime, because the air in the playground is not fit to breathe.

One of the chemicals belched out by every car's exhaust is lead—a deadly poison. Chemists employed by the oil companies tell us there is not enough of it to do us any harm. Others are not so optimistic.

In some Western countries people already have so much lead in their bloodstreams that they are halfway to the recognised poison level. Even at these lower levels, animals are known to die younger than they otherwise would.[1] What does this lead in our bodies do to our own health? Nobody knows, but it is hardly likely to do us much good.

Another poison that has been pumped into the air with careless abandon is DDT. For many years nobody realised that it *was* a poison. Then at last the penny dropped.

Millions of birds, fishes and wild animals died mysteriously, and their deaths were traced to DDT poisoning. A number of farm workers were made ill by it, and some actually died. In some places babies were harmed by the DDT in their mothers' milk.

Governments reacted firmly. Some countries, including Sweden and Canada, banned DDT altogether, and others have limited its use.

But this was shutting the menagerie door after the lion had bolted. DDT had already found its way into living things all over the world. Although no DDT had been used within a thousand miles, the fish in the central Atlantic and the penguins of Antarctica all carried their quota.

Because DDT is such a stable chemical it will be around for hundreds of years, even if we stop using it tomorrow. It is absorbed and retained by living things, and when one animal is eaten by another its store of DDT is passed on.

For this reason man himself is not immune.

Americans woke up one morning to find that their bodies were officially classed as unfit for human consumption! In the U.S.A. meat must not be sold if it contains more than 5 parts of DDT per million. But the flesh of the average American contains 10 parts per million of this poison. Their only consolation was that some other nations were much worse off: the typical inhabitant of India is carrying 29 parts per million within him.

Every year many new chemicals come on to the market. Many of them—drugs like thalidomide, pesticides like DDT, various ingredients of paint and plastics and petrol, and hosts of other substances—are eventually found to be harmful and have to be withdrawn.

The worrying thing is that it often takes years for the ill effects of these chemicals to be discovered. By that time untold harm may have been done. How many of the chemicals in regular use today are a menace to the future of mankind? Nobody knows for sure, but some of them may well be.

As Dr. David Price, an officer of the U.S. Public Health Service, has said, "We all live under the haunting fear that something may corrupt the environment to the point where man joins the dinosaurs as an obsolete form of life."[2]

The Not-So-Peaceful Atom

After the first atomic bombs were exploded, the atom was everybody's bogey-man. Gradually the fear wore off, and people learnt that the atom in peacetime could be a friend.

It could generate electricity and cure some kinds of cancer and find leaks in water pipes and do all manner of useful things. Atoms for Peace had arrived.

There was only one snag. Whenever you harness the atom to do a useful job, you can't help creating a great deal of radioactive waste. Disposing of this waste is a problem that scientists are at their wits' end trying to solve.

Just how worried they are can be seen from the remarks of James Schlesinger, the chairman of the Atomic Energy Commission in the U.S.A. In 1972 he suggested packing atomic waste into rockets and firing it into the sun!

Quite apart from its enormous cost, there is one great objection to this proposal. Every so often a rocket goes wrong, and has to be blown up in mid-air. The thought of this happening to a load of atomic poison is blood-curdling.

In the meantime the nuclear powers dispose of their rubbish as best they can. Some of it is dumped in the deepest parts of the sea. The theory is that the ocean currents will not bring it up to the surface again, but some scientists dispute this. They think there is a real risk that we may make the sea dangerously radioactive.

Much of America's nuclear waste is buried in the world's most expensive cemetery, at Hanford in the north-west of the United States. It covers 650 square miles—the size of a typical English county—and cost hundreds of millions of dollars to build.

Buried in the ground at Hanford are a number of enormous concrete vaults. Inside each vault is a steel cauldron filled with a fearful witch's brew—boiling radioactive liquid.

The vapour this gives off must not be allowed to escape, and so a mass of machinery works day and night to cool these vapours and return them to the cauldrons.

This burial ground with all its complex machinery must be kept going until long after its builders are all dead. Its contents will remain dangerous for centuries, even if no more is added to them. But in fact fresh radioactive waste is accumulating at an ever-increasing rate, and the shortage of burial plots is becoming acute.

To make matters worse, it was discovered in 1966 that the Hanford nuclear graveyard was built in the wrong place. A geological survey showed that the site was prone to earthquakes, one of which might split the tombs wide open and release their deadly contents.

It is impossible to say how serious a disaster this would cause. Experts estimate that there is already about a hundred million gallons of nuclear poison in store at Hanford and other disposal centres—enough to poison every man, woman and child on earth.

Although there is no likelihood that all this could be released at once, the amount in store is growing rapidly. So is the danger of a disastrous escape.

U Thant, the former Secretary General of the United Nations, was not exaggerating when he warned the world, "Life on earth as a whole may be threatened if pollution is not controlled."

Even the Mighty Ocean

More than three-quarters of the earth's surface is covered by sea. This is not just a waste of good land. The sea is there for a purpose. Without it, life on earth could not exist.

Our climate is governed by the sea. It keeps temperatures within the range that we can tolerate, and it provides the rainfall that prevents the earth from becoming one vast desert.

It has other, more subtle, functions. A large part of the oxygen we breathe is manufactured by the livings things within the sea. It receives waste products from the land, breaks them down, and through the activity of birds and animals and natural forces it returns many of them to the land.

Now Man is in danger of disrupting this age-old cycle of sea and land and air. One of the world's foremost oceanologists, Jacques Cousteau, has warned that the oceans will be dead in twenty years.

This may be an exaggerated estimate of the danger. But the problem is there nevertheless. We *are* poisoning the oceans, though it is anybody's guess how long they will take to die.

When Thor Heyerdahl crossed the Atlantic in 1969 on his papyrus raft, *Ra,* he complained that the ocean was one great sewer. Even in mid-Atlantic, more than a thousand miles from land, the water was so filthy that his men refused to fill their toothmugs with it. Much of the filth was recognisably of human origin.

Yet twenty years earlier, when he crossed the Pacific on another raft, *Kon-Tiki*, the ocean had been as clear as glass.

Some of the pollution is introduced directly from ships. About two million tons of oil enter the sea that way every year. But most of the filth in the oceans gets there through our habit of using rivers as sewers, and coastal waters as dumping grounds for rubbish.

In 1971 many Mediterranean bathing beaches had to be closed, because the high sewage content of the water was creating a health hazard. The same year an international conference of marine biologists concluded *unanimously* that marine life (not just in the Mediterranean, but everywhere) was in serious danger of destruction by pollution.

The Soil That Feeds Us

If you were to bore a hole to the centre of the earth it would be about twenty-one million feet deep. In all that distance you would find nothing but barren subsoil and rock, except in the top foot or so. (The actual thickness of the topsoil varies from place to place, but it averages about a foot.)

Everything we eat is grown in that thin top layer of fertile soil. Those twelve inches are all that stand between us and starvation. Yet in many parts of the world this precious layer is being worn away at an alarming rate. In some places as much as a third of an inch is disappearing every year.

Most of this vanishing topsoil is washed out to sea by rivers. Geologists calculate that about 24 thousand million tons are lost in this way every year, and that about half this total is directly due to Man's interference with Nature.

The other half—Nature's own contribution—does not matter, since new topsoil is being formed all the time. Until Man started to interfere, Nature was making new topsoil at just about the right rate to make up for the losses. But now that Man has altered the balance, the world's fertile soil is steadily getting thinner.

Man's interference with Nature takes many different forms.

We cut down trees and plant crops on hillsides where Nature intended that only trees should grow. But our crops cannot hold the soil together as Nature's trees did. Muddy torrents cascade down the slopes until nothing but bare rock remains.

Or we plough up the great prairies, where the soil and climate are suited for growing grass. Short-sighted methods of husbandry soon exhaust the soil, until the hot winds of summer are able to blow it away. The great dust bowls of the U.S.A. and Kazakhstan in the U.S.S.R. were created within living memory in this way.

Many tropical forests grow in a red soil called laterite. This is used in many countries for making roads, because when exposed to the weather it sets hard, almost like concrete.

Hard-pressed tropical farmers cut down forests and start cultivation. They soon have to admit defeat. After a few years they move on, leaving behind them a wilderness of rock-like laterite.

In other places men bring new lands into cultivation by great irrigation schemes. But all too often those schemes go wrong, and destroy the land they are supposed to improve.

This happened with the world's largest irrigation scheme, in the Indus valley in Pakistan. The engineers who designed it got their sums wrong. They failed to predict the outcome of inadequate drainage and a high rate of evaporation.

The consequences of their mistakes are now so plain that you can see them from an aircraft. Vast tracts of land are a shimmering wilderness of white, as desolate as the Arctic that they resemble. The whiteness is a film of salt, brought there in solution by the irrigation waters and left behind to sterilise the once fertile land.

Man Against the Desert

Adjoining every desert is a fringe of marginal land. In these dry areas a certain amount of vegetation grows. This is enough to support a limited number of wild or domestic animals. Unfortunately, herdsmen insist on introducing larger herds of goats and other animals than these marginal lands can sustain. The result is inevitable. The vegetation is destroyed, the soil disappears in sandstorms, and the desert moves in.

All told, Man has already turned about two million square miles of agricultural land into desert. That amounts to about one-thirtieth of the earth's entire land surface, or more than one-twentieth of the habitable parts of the earth.

It is tempting to think that we might be able to undo the harm we have done, or to reclaim some of the world's natural deserts. But in fact every attempt to improve on Nature is fraught with difficulty, as the following story shows.

Egypt's pride and joy is the new Aswan Dam. Its irrigation waters have brought large areas of new land into cultivation.

But the Egyptians are paying a heavy price for this new farmland. A great dam is a massive interference with Nature, and Nature has a habit of kicking back in unexpected ways.

Here are some of the unfortunate consequences

that are making some thoughtful Egyptians wonder if it would have been better never to have built the Aswan dam.

(1) The irrigated lands downstream of the dam are becoming less fertile. They are feeling the lack of the millions of tons of minerals that used to be brought down each year by the floodwaters of the Nile.

(2) The sardine fishermen of the eastern Mediterranean have been hard hit. The marine vegetation which once fed vast shoals of sardines is withering, for lack of the minerals formerly supplied by the Nile.

(3) The same minerals that are needed so badly below the dam are starting to silt up the lake behind the dam. Each year its storage capacity is reduced.

(4) Many thousands of Egyptians have been made seriously ill by the Aswan scheme. Its irrigation channels form a perfect breeding ground for water snails. These carry a parasite which gets into the bodies of people who come in contact with the water. This causes a highly unpleasant disease called bilharzia. It is practically incurable.

Hunger, Gnawing Hunger

Despite all that we have done to it, Britain is still a very pleasant place in which to live.

It is easy to forget that we have cut down most of our beautiful forests and killed off much of our wildlife. We needn't look at the ugly spoil heaps in our mining areas, or the foul slums of our big cities—unless, of course, we are unlucky enough to live there.

It's true that now and again life can be frustrating. When we are stuck in a traffic jam or blacked out by a power strike it is tempting to curse this complex civilisation of ours.

But most of the time life is enjoyable. We have lots of leisure and many pleasant ways of spending it. We have good homes filled with devices for making ourselves more comfortable.

We are not very often ill, and expert medical care is available when we are. Above all, we do not know what it is to feel really hungry.

If you have never been outside Europe you will find it hard to realise what life is like in Asia or Africa or South America.

One human being in every seven lives in India. It is worth making an effort to understand what it feels like to be a lower-class Indian.

To do this, imagine that you were born and bred in Calcutta. You were one of a family of twelve. Six of them died as children, but you were one of the lucky ones. You survived.

That doesn't mean you are healthy, though. You are probably infected with some horribly enervating disease, such as hookworm, or schistosomiasis, or malaria—or maybe even two or three of them at once. They will stay with you until the day you die.

If you are lucky, you live in a house—if you can call it a house. It is a good deal smaller than an Englishman's garage, and much less substantially built. You share it with seven other people.

The roof leaks. There is no water supply, no electricity, and no cooking facilities except a fire of dried cow dung just outside the door. For sanitation there is an open trench a few yards from the house.

In the monsoon season the whole district is flooded. Then you have to wade past your own floating excrement when you want to go out, and the floor of your house becomes a sea of mud.

You console yourself with the thought that others are worse off than yourself. Half a million inhabitants of Calcutta—yes, *half a million*—have no home at all.

They sleep in doorways, on railway platforms,

beneath parked cars—anywhere they can. Their only possessions are the ragged clothes they wear, and perhaps a battered cooking bowl.

You and they have one thing in common: hunger, everlasting gnawing hunger. A healthy human being needs 2,500 calories a day. Most Westerners eat rather more than this: the average American consumes 3,200 calories.

But a great many men have to get by on 2,000 calories. This is the average daily intake of the inhabitants of all the tropical countries lumped together. You, unfortunately, get much less than the average. In a good day you might manage 1,500 calories, or two half-decent one-course meals; at times you have to make do with one.

You weigh several stones less than your counterpart in Western Europe. Your resistance to disease is low, so that you are prone to catch one infection after another.

The miserable existence you call life is unlikely to last very long. You will probably die before you are fifty. There won't be a doctor present when you do. You may never even see a properly qualified medical man at any time in your life.

You are not alone in your misery. There are many millions just like you in India, and millions more in other countries. Hundreds of millions of black and brown and yellow peoples are very little better off than you are.

Such is this swinging, booming, raving, despairing world in which we live today.

Half of us are defiling this once-fair earth with the waste products of our affluence.

The other half eke out a squalid existence, in conditions that we wouldn't let our domestic pets endure.

2

WHERE ARE WE GOING?

The typical inhabitant of Calcutta might be excused for thinking that things couldn't possibly get any worse.

But he would be wrong. Things could be far worse, even in Calcutta. And there is every indication that they are going to become worse—very much worse.

The trouble is that the population of India is increasing at a fantastic rate. Despite all the illness and premature deaths in India, its population looks like doubling during the next thirty years.

That means an extra five hundred million Indians to feed and clothe and house by the year 2000.

India is by no means exceptional. The population of the world as a whole is also expected to double during the next thirty to thirty-five years. That means another three thousand million human beings to be provided for by the end of this century.

How are we going to feed all those extra people?

The simple answer is that we can't.

As a matter of fact we cannot even feed properly all the people in the world today. To do that we should need a sudden ten per cent increase in world food production, and an enormous improvement in our methods of distributing it.

That would bring us up to date with the world's present population. But after that we should have to go on increasing food production at the same rate as the population—two and a half per cent per year.

It's not only extra food that is needed. Our new

neighbours also require clothing, housing, transport, and all the other necessities of life.

Just to maintain the present pathetic standards in India (and a great many other tropical countries) the government there is faced with an impossible task. Within thirty years they would need to double the number of houses, schools, roads, wells, shops, and everything else.

Judging by past performance it just can't be done. The standard of living in the city slums of India has been falling for years. All the indications are that it will keep on falling.

The Stork Versus the Plough

Mass hunger is nothing new. All through history the human race has lived on the edge of famine.

As the population of the world has grown, Man's need for extra food has been met in one of two ways. New lands have been brought under cultivation, or new methods of agriculture have been introduced.

The need to keep increasing food production to keep pace with population pressures has been called "the race of the stork against the plough".

Unfortunately it is a race that the plough cannot possibly win. As the philosopher Malthus realised two hundred years ago, the power of the plough is limited but the power of the stork is unlimited.

The plough obtained a clear lead during the nineteenth century, when the vast new farmlands of North America were opened up. This was followed by another big advance in the early part of the twentieth century, when artificial fertilisers became widely used.

Then agricultural progress slowed up a little, and the stork began to gain ground. Fortunately the plough made a fresh spurt in the nineteen sixties, with the introduction of "miracle wheat" and "miracle rice".

These are grains with a far heavier yield than the old

varieties. But the farmer has to pay for his bigger crops. The "miracle" grains need many times as much fertiliser as the old varieties. They are also more liable to attack by diseases and pests.

It begins to look as if the plough has made its last really big advance. There is practically no more good agricultural land waiting to be developed. Within a few years all the land that can be ploughed will be ploughed

Agricultural science will doubtless make further progress. But there is bound to be a limit to the amount of food that can be grown on an acre of land. As we get closer to that limit scientists will find themselves making smaller and smaller steps forward.

Meanwhile the stork is flying as strongly as ever. Within a few years it will have left the plough far behind. The titles of several recent books warn us what will happen then:

The Hungry Future[1]
Who Will Eat?[2]
Famine, 1975[3]
The Hungry Planet[4]
Can Britain Survive?[5]
The Death of Tomorrow[6]
The Doomsday Book[7]
The Closing Circle[8]
Planet in Peril?[9]
Only One Earth[10]

These books are not the productions of a few cranks. The writers are all responsible men and women, and some of them are distinguished scholars.

The last two books on the list were actually commissioned by the United Nations. You could hardly have a more authoritative expression of world opinion than a book backed by UNO. And yet these two books sound the alarm as clearly as the rest.

A Twentieth-century Prodigal Son

Remember the story of the Prodigal Son?

He was given a fortune by his father. It was his inheritance, paid in advance—a once-and-for-all gift.

He could have been wise and put it in the bank. It would have provided him with a sizeable income for the rest of his life. But he didn't. He "wasted his substance in riotous living".

Before long he was living among the pigs, hungry and miserable.

The developed nations are at present engaged in a gorgeous spending spree, like the Prodigal in his heyday. As a British prime minister told his voters a few years ago, "You've never had it so good!"

America is away out in front in this great race to have a good time. To keep up this position every single American has to burn thirteen tons of coal each year, or its equivalent in other types of fuel.

In 1968 the average American had three hundredweights of copper, three hundredweights of lead, two hundredweights of aluminium, two hundredweights of zinc and ten tons of steel in use at any one time.[11] In 1967 he was spending £40 a year on furniture and nearly as much on clothing.[12]

These figures are based on the latest statistics available to me. But they are hopelessly out of date, because the quantities were increasing every year until 1974. And the countries of Western Europe and Japan are not so very far behind in the standard-of-living race.

Our modern way of life depends upon three things: power, metals, and chemicals. Where do they all come from?

Our power supplies come mainly from coal and

oil—especially oil—with a small contribution from hydro-electric schemes and atomic power stations.

Metals are provided by a worldwide army of miners, working day and night to try and keep up with the developed world's ever-increasing demands.

Chemicals come from a wide variety of sources. A very large number of vital chemicals are produced from oil. A great many others are dug out of the earth, or extracted from other materials that have been mined.

In short, our whole civilisation is totally dependent upon the earth's mineral resources.

Going, Going . . .

How long are these going to last? How long before the twentieth-century Prodigal Son finds himself bankrupt, and sorrowfully descends to the level of the pigs?

If you have ever driven through Cornwall you will know that mineral reserves can run out with dramatic suddenness. The Cornish countryside is littered with the remains of old tin mines. In 1800 half the entire world supply of tin came from those underground treasure houses. By 1900 they were shut down, exhausted.

Obviously the world's supplies of minerals are not going to vanish all at once. Some things are going to run out sooner than others. But we shall certainly start to feel the pinch within the present century.

It looks as if all our silver, gold, mercury, lead, platinum, tin and zinc could be gone before the year 2000. Copper and tungsten will probably follow soon after, and throughout the next century one metal after another is likely to disappear.[13]

"Don't worry," say the optimists. "We shall probably find vast new sources of supply before then."

"That's rather unlikely," reply the geologists. "We've already scoured the earth for likely deposits, and if we do find any unexpected reserves they will only stave off the evil day for a few years."

"Well, we'll just have to use substitutes," reply the optimists. "You know—plastics and things."

Poor, misguided optimists! Technologists know only too well that some of these metals have unique properties. There simply is no substitute for them.

As for plastics, they too will be on the disappearing list within the lifetime of people born today. Most plastics are made from oil. And, as the president of a great American chemical corporation said in 1972, "There is no substitute, now or in the foreseeable future, for petroleum [as a source of] the great bulk of synthetic organic chemicals and plastics."[14]

Petroleum, the lifeblood of our civilisation. We depend upon it for power, for transport, for plastics, and a whole host of essential chemicals.

And the world is running out of it—fast.

One of the most eminent bodies of scientists in the world is the National Research Council of the U.S. Academy of Sciences. In 1970 this Council declared that nine-tenths of the world's recoverable petroleum would be used up within sixty-five years. Their estimate made a generous allowance for all the new oilfields likely to be discovered in the meantime.

Shortages Begin

The year 1973 was a turning point in human history.

Experts had known for a long time that shortages of vital raw materials were on the way. But now, for the first time, the ordinary man realised that the earth's resources were limited. All over the world, in rich and poor countries alike, people's living standards were hit by the shortage of petroleum.

We are all too familiar with the effects upon the rich countries: inflation, a fall in trade, unemployment, and an increase in strikes and social unrest. But the poverty-stricken nations of the Third World suffered the worst.

They have had to reduce their purchases of highly priced fuel for farm tractors. Fertilizer, too, is in short supply and its price has tripled. These factors, along with a spell of appalling weather, have led to decreased harvests. Yet every year the Third World has fifty million more mouths to feed.

At the United Nations World Food Conference, held in Rome in November 1974, a gloomy picture was unveiled. World food stocks had fallen to a perilously low level. Four hundred and sixty million people were already existing on the brink of starvation, and there was little hope of improving their condition.

The long-term prospects are bleak indeed. The nations holding reserves of scarce minerals will want to get every penny they can for them. Prices will continue to rise, and more and more goods will become scarce. A few lucky nations may manage to maintain their present living standards for a time, but most countries are likely to grow poorer and poorer.

Can It Really Be True?

The natural reaction on being told facts like this is to disbelieve them. Can they possibly be true?

If so, why haven't the scientists warned us long ago? They must have seen it coming.

The answer is quite simple. Human beings never did like facing up to unpleasant facts. Men of great foresight are generally ignored, or ridiculed, or even persecuted, when they warn their fellows that trouble is coming.

This happened to Sir Winston Churchill in the nineteen-thirties. He was one of the few Englishmen of his day who could see further than his nose.

He warned his fellow-countrymen, time and again,

that Hitler was bent on conquest. Hardly anybody listened to him. People preferred to believe Chamberlain, who declared in 1938 (against all the evidence) that it would be "Peace in our time"!

There is a word for far-sighted people who insist that trouble is on the way. We call them "Jeremiahs", after the Jewish prophet who foretold the conquest of Jerusalem by the Babylonians.

When we use this word we usually forget one thing. *Jeremiah was right.*

His prophecies were fulfilled to the letter. The city was conquered, as he said. Those people who followed his advice escaped with their lives. Those who took refuge in wishful thinking were caught unprepared and suffered miserably.

All through history the Jeremiahs have usually been right, even when they have been in a very small minority. Today the Jeremiahs are not just a few unimportant people. The warnings of world catastrophe today come from the very top.

Thousands of prominent scientists have expressed their concern. So have public figures like the Duke of Edinburgh and cabinet minister Mr. Peter Walker.

The United Nations called a major international conference at Stockholm in 1972, to bring the world's plight to the attention of the world's statesmen. As a direct consequence the British Government set up a research unit to study the dangers, and to advise on how to meet them.

Doomwatching, as the cynics call it, is no longer a joke. It is a very serious affair, a concern of governments and nations.

It is a matter of life and death to the whole human race. If people are determined enough they may be able to pretend for a few more years that the problem does not exist. But not for long.

Sooner or later it will force itself upon the attention of

us all in a most unpleasant manner. When that happens how are people likely to react?

It is always difficult to predict human behaviour. Before attempting to answer this question we must look at another aspect of modern life.

Living in Cities

One day in 1972 I had dinner with a visiting scientist from New York.

"I don't know what's come over the old city," he lamented. "It always was an unsafe place for a woman to go about alone at night. But now it isn't safe for a woman to walk about downtown New York alone at any hour of the *day*!"

He was not exaggerating. Crime in New York has broken all records lately. At times it looks as if law and order is about to break down altogether. The city has become so hard to govern that its mayoralty has been called "the worst job in the world".

New York is not all that exceptional. There are areas in Glasgow, just a few miles from my home, where I would not care to walk after dark—not even in company with several friends.

In the American city of St. Louis there was once a multi-million-dollar complex of tall flats, called Pruitt-Igoe. They are there no more.

Within a few years this group of fine modern buildings became such a lawless jungle that people were afraid to live there. The city council was forced to declare the scheme a total loss, dynamite the abandoned tower blocks, and clear the site.

There is no doubt that city living brings out the worst in people. Statistics show that the crime rate in the big towns of America is several times as great as in the small towns.[15] During 1972, one-third of all the inhabitants of the central areas of America's cities were victims of crime.[16]

Cities breed mental illness as well as crime. One research worker found that neurosis was more common in people who lived in flats than in those who lived in houses with gardens. The higher up they lived in their block of flats, the more likely they were to become mentally ill.[17]

Many experiments have been carried out on laboratory animals to investigate the results of unnatural living conditions. These all point to the same conclusion.

When any animals are walled up together in large numbers they start to act as if they were crazy. They stop behaving like animals and descend to low tricks that only human beings are normally capable of: rape, robbery with violence, and savaging their own babies.

It seems clear that neither men nor animals were meant to live in big cities. They certainly have to suffer for it if they choose to do so.

Yet cities still seem to draw men like magnets. Especially in the poorer countries cities are growing at an almost unbelievable rate. Calcutta, for example, had between one and one-and-a-half million inhabitants in 1930, but is approaching ten million today.

Two hundred years ago probably ninety-nine per cent of the world's population lived in villages. Today well over half the people in the developed countries live in towns, and over a quarter in great cities with more than half a million inhabitants.

This may be one reason why the world is rapidly becoming more and more criminal, more and more violent. It is a sad reflection on the world's richest country that more American children under five are battered to death by a parent or guardian than die from tuberculosis, whooping cough, polio, measles, diabetes, rheumatic fever and appendicitis combined.[18]

A few years ago the Montreal City Police went on strike for one day. Thousands of citizens immediately went on the rampage, fighting and vandalising and looting. Two people were killed, a thousand plate glass windows were broken, a million dollars' worth of goods and a vast amount of money was stolen—within a few hours!

Evidently modern Man—city-dwelling Man, at least—is a violent creature at heart. When the forces restraining him are taken away, he reacts violently.

Already the constraints of religion and public opinion have been largely whittled away. All that is left to keep man in check is the law.

It almost seems as if the human race is like one great volcano, ready to erupt when the opportunity arises.

The Ultimate Peril

Most of us like to think that the danger of a third world war is past.

Unfortunately there is no real ground for such a comforting belief. It is true that there may be little danger of a clash between East and West just at present. According to Harrison Salisbury, what we should fear most is "The Coming War Between Russia and China"—to quote the title of his widely circulated book.[19]

Three things referred to in this chapter will increase the likelihood of a major war as years go by: population pressure, diminishing resources, and increasingly violent behaviour by mankind.

Until 1974 only a handful of wealthy nations had the power to start a nuclear war. Then India exploded her first atomic bomb, and it was rumoured that Israel had secretly acquired a nuclear striking force. Within a few years several of the less developed countries are likely to possess atomic bombs. And they will probably be hungrier then than they are now, and angrier.

The major powers will certainly not use their most powerful weapons except as a last resort. It would be suicidal to do so. But angry, hungry men are not above doing crazy things.

Just what are these weapons that we hope will never be used?

Everybody knows about The Bomb. There are enough of those in store, according to Lord Ritchie-Calder, to provide every man, woman and child on earth with the equivalent of one hundred tons of TNT apiece.[20] An all-out nuclear war would certainly destroy our civilisation, and probably destroy mankind entirely.

But there are other weapons almost as horrible, and, according to many authorities, much more likely to be used.[21,22] Specially cultivated plant diseases could be loosed on an enemy's crops, starving him into submission. Plague germs could be quietly spread over Britain without anybody noticing it had happened—until an epidemic carried off half our population within a week.

Weapons like this do not belong to science fiction. They already exist in several countries. They are kept in readiness. They could, if deemed necessary, be used tomorrow.

Why Nothing Gets Done

One of the silliest advertisements I have ever seen appeared—of all places—in a recent issue of a scientific journal.

The whole-page spread was put out by one of Britain's greatest aircraft companies, and it said in large letters:

> "Many scientists and ecologists believe that the better management of the resources of our planet, and the eventual control of pollution and other such ills, depends upon the ready access to Space afforded by the Space Shuttle."[23]

I don't blame the British Aircraft Corporation for

wanting to push the Space Shuttle project. The British aircraft industry is in a bad way. A lot of jobs probably depend upon this project going ahead. But it is a pity that they think their cause will be helped by publishing this ludicrous statement.

No doubt many scientists can be found who do believe such nonsense. Most of those whose jobs are at stake would probably give their assent.

Almost every other well-informed person would recognise it as the exact opposite of the truth. The Space Shuttle is a cross between a moon rocket and a supersonic aircraft. It will not promote the "better management" of our planet's dwindling resources. On the contrary, it will squander them at a fantastic rate. As for furthering the "control of pollution", it is more likely to win a prize for polluting.

It is easy to see why nothing much gets done to avert the global crisis. There is always somebody whose private interests clash with the interests of the planet as a whole.

In the case just quoted, it is the aircraft industry that stands to gain a lot from the Space Shuttle. The rest of the human race stands to lose immeasurably from it.

Unfortunately it is politicians that make the decisions upon which the future of the planet will depend. And politicians are all too easily pushed around by groups with vested interests.

Politicians can always find plenty of experts to say what they want them to say. When President Eisenhower wanted to carry on with nuclear tests he announced in October 1956, "The continuance of the present rate of H-bomb testing by the most sober and responsible scientific judgement ... *does not imperil the health of humanity.*"[24]

Yet when President Johnson wanted to stop nuclear testing he said in October 1964, "This treaty [the nuclear test ban treaty] has halted the steady, menacing increase of radioactive fall-out. . . . Radioactive poisons were beginning *to threaten the safety of the people throughout the world.*"[24] [The italics in both quotations are mine.]

Most people who have studied the facts know that we are plunging headlong towards global disaster. They can see what needs to be done to save mankind from destroying itself. The Duke of Edinburgh put it very simply in a speech at Edinburgh University in 1969:

> "The process of destroying our natural environment is increasing with deadly momentum. . . . The fact is that we have the choice of human prosperity, on one hand, or human existence on this earth, on the other hand. If we think only of human prosperity we will certainly destroy the earth for hundreds of millions of years."[25]

That's it, then. In a nutshell, this is our choice: belt-tightening, or mass destruction.

In 1972 a team of prominent British scientists spelt it out in greater detail, in their "Blueprint for Survival".[13] Among other things they called upon Britain to:

(1) Stop using dangerous pesticides and excessive quantities of chemical fertiliser. (That would put up the cost of food.)

(2) Impose new taxes to discourage the use of raw material, fuels and electricity. (That would put up the price of everything else.)

(3) Stop building roads and restrict the use of cars.

(4) Spend vast sums of British taxpayers' money on increased aid to poverty-stricken countries overseas.

It is good to see someone being constructive. Measures like that—and a lot more besides—are certainly needed. But can you see such a programme ever getting off the ground?

If politicians took up the idea seriously, you might see a leaflet like this at the next general election:

> VOTE FOR JOE BLOGGS
>
> and the Save-the-World Party!
>
> **The other parties are leading you to World Disaster**
>
> WE OFFER:
>
> *Higher taxes*
> *Higher prices*
> *A lower standard of living*
> *Less fun*
>
> **AND A HOPE OF LIFE FOR YOUR GREAT-GRANDCHILDREN**

Can you imagine the remarks that would float around, as Mr. Bloggs lost his deposit?

"Bother the great-grandchildren! I want my new Ford, and I want it now."

No politician would dream of taking strong measures to avert some far-off, future calamity. All our major political parties are publicly committed to giving us more and more prosperity—and thus to bringing on the world crisis as soon as possible. The world's governments will not even consider taking drastic action until disaster starts to bite.

And by then it will be too late to do anything about it.

For reasons like this many people have abandoned hope. Albert Schweitzer spoke for them when he lamented, "Man has lost the capacity to foresee and to forestall. He will end by destroying the earth."[26]

Was Schweitzer right? Or is there still a hope for the future of our race?

Yes, there is one real ray of hope—but only one.

It is Planet Earth's last hope.

3

POST-MORTEM

Well, what went wrong? How did the world get into this frightening predicament? Is it possible to pin the blame on any particular class of people? Or are we all to blame? Or is it nobody's fault, but just mankind's bad luck that we have been faced with a situation beyond our power to control?

If only we knew the answers to these questions we might know what to do for the best. Discovering how you got into a mess is the first, essential step to getting out again. Unfortunately, the world's leaders cannot agree among themselves on how the world went wrong. And they show no sign of being able to put things right.

The sad fact is that the wisest men on earth are baffled. They are far-sighted enough to know that catastrophe is fast approaching, but they cannot see how to avert it.

A fresh approach to the problem is needed, desperately. It is not hard to find one. One source of information has always been neglected by most of the world's leaders.

It is a book called the Bible.

Thousands of years ago, this book showed men how to live in harmony with the rest of creation. By disregarding the book's advice modern Man has ravished Nature and brought the present crisis upon himself. But it is not too late to learn from our mistakes. By looking closely at the Bible it is possible to discover where we went wrong, and to see where the best hope for the future lies.

Genesis and the Population Explosion

Before Man began to interfere with Nature there was

nothing much wrong with Planet Earth. Nature was in a remarkably well-balanced condition which could have continued more or less indefinitely. Biologists have only recently discovered just how perfectly balanced Nature is, and a whole new branch of science—ecology—has had to be established to take account of this fact. And about time, too, say those scientists who know how often in the past we have blundered in our dealings with Nature.

When officials from the World Health Organisation launched an operation to prevent malaria in the Philippines, they never expected to cause a plague of rats. They thought their work would be finished when their insecticide had wiped out the mosquitoes.

What they never allowed for was the cockroaches, who feasted on the dead mosquitoes and accumulated large quantities of insecticide in their bodies. The cockroaches were eaten by lizards, which promply died. Domestic cats are not overfed in the Philippines, and they seized their opportunities to fill their stomachs with the poisonous bodies of the lizards. When the cats were all dead the rats multiplied exceedingly, and posed the harassed public health officials with another problem.

But an epidemic of rats is only a very small problem, compared with the epidemic of people that we call the population explosion. To see this in its proper setting we need to go back to the Book of Genesis.

When the creation of the world was complete, "God saw everything that He had made, and behold, it was very good." (Gen. 1:31.) As a self-sustaining system the world was ideal. Man was not yet a sinner, and not under sentence of death. Neither had he begun to reproduce his kind. Momentarily, the human population of the world was static, and hence in a state of balance.

Then, as a New Testament writer puts it, "Sin came into the world through one man and death through sin, and so death spread to all men." (Rom. 5:12.) If this had been the only change, Nature's balance would have been destroyed. So God took pains to preserve the balance, by introducing a second change at the same time. He said:

(1) "Thou shalt surely die . . . dust thou art, and unto dust shalt thou return." (Gen. 2:17 and 3:19, AV.)

(2) "I will greatly multiply thy sorrow and thy conception." (Gen. 3:16, AV.)

Whether you regard Adam and Eve as real people (as Jesus did, and as I do) or as symbols of the human race, the message of these words is clear. God arranged that "sorrow"—a word that embraces all forms of pain, and death—and "conception" would keep in step. Before man was sentenced to death, there was no conception. Afterwards, death and sorrow abounded, but human fertility was also multiplied.

Thus the balance in God's creation was preserved. In a primitive society a woman would have perhaps ten children, but seven of them might die in infancy. The population of the world did not stand still, but it increased only very slowly until about the middle of the last century.

Then the picture began to change. Until that time doctors were only available for the rich, and their powers were very limited. The nursing profession did not exist. Hospitals were little more than places where men and women went to die, unless they were lucky enough to pull round by the strength of their own constitutions.

But then medicine started to change from an art into a science. New knowledge, new tools and new drugs were placed into the hands of doctors. A steady stream of highly-trained physicians and surgeons poured out of our universities. Many of them went to the underdeveloped countries and began to reduce their death rates drastically.

Had they been able at the same time to reduce the reproduction rates of their patients, all would have been well. The balance established in Genesis would have been maintained with "sorrow" and "conception" still matched.

But this they could not do. They lacked the facilities. Even if they had been able to dispense family planning appliances, they would not have known how to persuade people to use them. In any case, they were blissfully unaware of the need to keep a balance between death and conception.

In addition, many of them were victims of their own religious prejudices against contraception. The Bible strongly condemns every form of immorality. But it never says that family planning is wrong, or forbids married couples to practise it.

This is not because birth control was unknown in Bible times. Far from it: Jewish women used to use primitive contraceptives at the time the New Testament was being written. Yet the New Testament writers did not blame them for doing so. If only religious leaders would be guided by the Bible they would not oppose birth control.

Now, at last, men are beginning to face the facts. Many people are aware that the population of the world is rocketing, and that, if this goes on, there will be seven thousand million hungry people in the world by the year 2000. In theory, most people agree that something should be done to limit the world's population. But nobody has yet come up with a practical suggestion for doing so.

The root of the trouble is that Man just isn't clever enough. He is proud of his ability to control atoms and molecules, and to put men on the moon. But when it comes to controlling human behaviour, Man is a mere child. He doesn't know where to begin.

We must, then, list the lack of human wisdom as

Problem Number One. Man was not wise enough to see that he was creating a population explosion. Now that we have done it, and can see what is causing the explosion, we are still not wise enough to know how to control it.

So, for survival, we need more wisdom, lots more—and we need it right now.

World's Most Destructive Animal

At the entrance to a bird sanctuary in Gloucestershire a mirror has been erected. Against it is this sign:

> "Look into the glass below and you will see a specimen of the most dangerous and destructive animal the world has ever known."

A grim sort of joke, thinks the visitor, as he looks at his own reflection.

Yet the facts speak for themselves. The museums of the world abound with stuffed specimens of extinct birds. Nearly all of them would be thriving today, if it were not for Man's destructive hand.

In the nineteenth century the skies of North America were darkened by great flocks of passenger pigeons. At the same time the cliffs encircling the North Atlantic were the breeding ground for millions of great auks.

Nowadays both these birds are "as dead as the dodo"—itself another victim of the rush to get cheap meat and eggs. Over seventy species of animal and bird have become extinct since 1900. A thousand others are on the danger list.

While some men are now anxious to preserve the species that still survive, others carry on in the same old way. In 1971 a detachment of troops from the British army were called out for guard duty in a Scottish forest. Their mission? To protect an osprey's nest that had been robbed by egg-thieves the year before.

It is a good sign that governments are now trying to protect wildlife from extinction. But animal- and bird-lovers complain that government measures are inadequate, and have come too late. There is no excuse for this lateness. A law for the protection of birds was in operation three thousand years ago:

> "If you chance to come upon a bird's nest, in any tree or on the ground, with young ones or eggs and the mother sitting upon the young or upon the eggs, you shall not take the mother with the young; *you shall let the mother go,* but the young you may take to yourself; that it may go well with you, and that you may live long." (Deut. 22 : 6, 7.)

In these words the Bible legislated against human greed. If the allegedly Christian peoples of Western Europe had obeyed the letter of God's law, many of our extinct birds would still be thriving. If they had tried to keep its spirit, many other species of birds and animals would have survived as well.

For the essence of the commandment quoted above, and of numerous others, is this: "Don't be greedy. In the long run it doesn't pay."

The same principle was expressed in another biblical law:

> "When you come into the land which I give you, the land shall keep a sabbath to the Lord. Six years you shall sow your field, and six years you shall prune your vineyard, and gather in its fruits; but in the seventh year there shall be a sabbath of solemn rest for the land, a sabbath to the Lord; you shall not sow your field or prune your vineyard." (Lev. 25 : 2–4.)

With modern methods of agriculture there is no need to let land lie fallow occasionally. But in earlier days this was often the only way to preserve the fertility of the soil.

When farmers ruthlessly cropped their fertile lands year after year, in disregard or ignorance of God's warning, they turned them into a wilderness. Many of the deserts of North Africa and the Middle East were formed in this way. These ruined lands are permanent monuments to Man's folly and greed.

Many scientists are now coming to recognise the Bible's wisdom in these matters. It would be an understatement to describe the biologist René Dubos as eminent. At the last count twenty-three different universities had given him honorary degrees. Yet he is not ashamed to go to the Book of Genesis for instruction.

He has pointed out that when Man was placed in the Garden of Eden, God told him *to till it and to keep it.* (Gen. 2:15.) This, commented Dubos, means that mankind must be concerned with what happens to the earth.[1]

Right at the start God told Man to look after his land. But all through history he has greedily exploited and plundered it.

Now that it is thousands of years too late, our race is beginning to realise the consequences of disobeying God's wise commandment.

The Road to Ruin

In the New Testament we find the same warning against greed.

> "For the love of money is the root of all evils . . . Those who desire to be rich fall into temptation, into a snare, into many senseless and hurtful desires that *plunge men into ruin and destruction.*" (1 Tim. 6:10, 9.)

Ruin and destruction. That's what greed leads to, says Paul. He was thinking primarily of individuals. But it is just as true of our whole technological civilisation. We are steadily ruining the beautiful planet we inhabit, destroying the world that gives us life, in our headlong pursuit of a higher standard of living.

Why have we stripped two-thirds of the world's forests of their trees, without replacing them? Because it is cheaper to plunder than to replant.

Why is every mining area in the world disfigured by spoil heaps? Because it costs money to put the spoil where it belongs, back under the earth.

Why are factory chimneys allowed to belch out smoke and dust, and the exhausts of vehicles permitted to emit harmful gases? Our engineers know exactly how to stop this filth from getting into the air and damaging our lungs. Just one thing prevents them from doing so: money. We could have clean air tomorrow—at a price. But we prefer to put up with smogs and bronchitis, and remain that little bit richer.

We discharge raw sewage into rivers and lakes and coastal waters, with reckless disregard of animal life and human health. There is no need for this filthy habit. We could dispose of all our sewage hygienically if we wished. But that would be expensive. So we choose to have an affluent, effluent society.

It rarely seems to occur to Christians that pollution is an offence against God. But it is. In the far-off days before factories were invented, carelessly handled sewage was the only serious form of pollution. God laid down a law for its proper disposal:

> "You shall have a place outside the camp and you shall go out to it; and you shall have a stick with your weapons; and when you sit down outside, you shall dig a hole with it, and turn back and cover up your excrement ... *your camp must be holy.*" (Deut. 23:12–14.)

God required His people to live in holy, unpolluted surroundings. His world was very good and they were not to spoil it with their filth. Life would be much more pleasant for all of us if only modern nations tried to obey the Bible's basic rule of hygiene.

So the Bible points us to a second major cause of our crisis. The culprit is human greed, or "the profit motive" as we politely term it today. Unless we can learn to do what is best instead of what is most profitable, our unhappy society will destroy itself. This the Bible clearly warns us, if we will listen.

The other great curse of our civilisation is war. For many centuries men have wondered: what causes it? Nobody has yet produced a better answer than that given in the Bible:

> "What causes wars, and what causes fightings among you? Is it not your passions that are at war in your members? You desire and do not have; so you kill. And you covet and cannot obtain; so you fight and wage war." (Jas. 4:1, 2.)

Once again we are back at our starting point. The love of money is the root of all evils, and that includes war. Rather than go short, men are prepared to fight, and kill, and die.

If human greed causes war, even in times of plenty, the prospects for the future are bleak indeed. Every year there are 70 million more mouths to feed—and hardly any new farmland with which to feed them. The oil that drives our farm tractors is fast being used up.

One day the nations that are now rich will become poor. They will then be faced with a tragic choice: starve, or fight. When that happens, even the fear of the atom bomb is not likely to hold them back.

What the World Needs

Perhaps you think that the Bible has not told us anything new.

After all, the Bible only tells us what leading conservationists have been saying for years. Our two big enemies are human folly and human greed. Unless we can learn to overcome them, we shall destroy the earth and ourselves along with it. Man must learn to respect Nature, to live in harmony with it instead of plundering it and polluting it.

This sounds like simple common sense. The one surprising thing about it is this: the wisest men of Europe and America only started saying it within the last few years. *But the Bible began to say it more than three thousand years ago.*

A book so far ahead of its time must surely be in a class of its own. We have seen how the Bible anticipated our troubles, and even laid down rules that might have kept us out of trouble if we had obeyed them. Does it have anything to say about our prospects of escaping world-wide disaster? Because, if so, its views obviously deserve a careful examination.

In fact the Bible has a great deal to say about the calamity the world is heading for, and of the only possible way out. The rest of this book will explain what it tells us.

4

THE ONLY WAY OUT

The solution is ridiculously simple.

What we need is a central government, a good one, to rule wisely over the whole world.

That would solve all our problems. This world government, if it existed, would compel men to act sensibly. It would curb human greed at all levels. Individuals would not be allowed to damage our environment in pursuit of their own selfish interests. Big companies would be prevented from making quick profits at the expense of the public. Nations would have to pull together: there would be no trade wars, no cold war, no fear of world war.

Sounds lovely, doesn't it? What a pity there are so many obstacles to prevent it coming about.

The most obvious snag is that such a government has never existed, and, it would seem, is never likely to. Nations are very jealous of their sovereignty. No national government would dream of surrendering its authority to a world government.

Also, it would be impossible to reach agreement on what kind of government the world should have. America and Western Europe would fight to the death with atomic weapons, rather than submit to a communist world government. They agree with Bertrand Russell, that:

> "The next war, if it comes, will be the greatest disaster that will have befallen the human race up to that moment. I can think of only one greater disaster: the extension of the Kremlin's power over the whole world."[1]

In the same way, Russia and China would undoubtedly regard a third world war as the lesser of two evils, if it came to a choice between that and giving up communism.

Then there is the biggest snag of all. What we need is a wise, benevolent world government. A bad world government would be worse than no world government at all. And if we had a world government it would certainly be unfit for its task.

Why, we human beings are not even capable of directing our own individual lives adequately! What chance has any man, or group of men, of being able to rule the whole world wisely and benevolently?

Situation Vacant

Let's try to draw up a job specification for a world ruler, to see what sort of man he would have to be. An advertisement for the post might read like this:

> *WORLD PRESIDENT. Applications are invited for the most important job in the world.*
>
> *The successful candidate will need to be an altogether exceptional man. He must know all the answers. He will have to wrestle with the world's trickiest problems and come up with the right solution every time.*
>
> *He must have the personality to inspire devoted loyalty in his subordinates, and the strength of character to impose his decisions (some of which are bound to be highly unpopular) on the whole world. He must be capable of directing the powerful World Police Force without being the least bit tyrannical or ruthless.*
>
> *His personal conduct must be spotless. He must show the world that his policies are good by setting a superb example of unselfishness. Whilst being free from human weakness himself, he must be kind and understanding*

when he is confronted with those weaknesses in other people.

The successful candidate will receive a salary appropriate to the post—that is to say, nothing. The right man will do the work for the love of mankind, without wanting any material reward for it.

There is only one man who could meet that specification, or anything like it.

The advertisement is a description of Jesus Christ!

He certainly knows all the answers. Even while He shared our mortal nature Jesus had a great reputation as a problem-solver. When a domestic crisis occurred at a place called Cana His mother told the servants, "Do whatever he tells you." (John 2:5.) Evidently her experience had taught her what to do when an insoluble problem arose: "Just leave it to Jesus. He is never at a loss."

As for His powers of leadership, the world has never seen anyone like Him. Far more men have laid down their lives willingly for His sake than for any other leader. When Jesus made His last journey to Judea, where certain death awaited Him, the reaction of Thomas was typical: "Let us also go, that we may die with him." (John 11:16.)

Enforcing His decisions would be no problem. Even while He was still a mortal man the force of His personality was awe-inspiring. A detachment of armed guards was once sent to arrest Him. They came back empty-handed, pleading, "No man ever spoke like this man!" (John 7:46.)

Since then, His power has been greatly increased. After His resurrection He declared, "All authority in heaven and on earth has been given to me." (Matt. 28:18.)

No one will be able to criticise His behaviour. While He was on earth He threw out a challenge to His opponents. "Which one of you can prove that I am guilty of sin?" (John 8:46, Today's English Version.) Although they hated Jesus they could never take up His challenge.

But although He never knew what it was to sin, He can still sympathise with us when we slip up. As the New Testament puts it:

> "Our high priest is not one who cannot feel sympathy with our weaknesses. On the contrary, we have a high priest that was tempted in every way that we are, but did not sin." (Heb. 4:15, Today's English Version.)

Above all, Jesus Christ is the only great figure in all history who was completely untainted by the love of greatness or of power, or of material possessions. He refused to let His admirers make Him a king or even to call Him "Good Teacher". (John 6:15; Mark 10:17.) Where earthly possessions were concerned Jesus was on a par with the birds and the wild animals. (Luke 9:58.)

He never did anything just to gratify His own desires. His every action was calculated to please His Father. (John 6:38.)

Without any doubt, the Lord Jesus Christ is the only man who would make a satisfactory world president. He would be ideal for the job. The only question is this: would He be willing to take it on?

God Makes a Promise

One thing at least is certain. Jesus has not left the earth for ever. He is coming back, one day.

It sometimes seems as if only a few insignificant little sects believe this. But that is not so. The Roman Catholic Church officially believes in the Second Coming. So do the Church of England, the Baptists, the Presbyterians, and nearly every other denomination of note. Every Christian worthy of the name is supposed to accept the Apostles' Creed:

> "I believe in God the Father . . . and in Jesus Christ . . . He ascended into heaven, and sitteth on the right hand of God the Father Almighty; *from thence He shall come* to judge the quick and the dead."

It would be very difficult for any of the major churches to reject the doctrine of the Second Coming, since they all publicly declare their belief in the Bible. And the whole New Testament, from Matthew to Revelation, is full of the teaching that Jesus will return to the earth.

At the very moment that Jesus ascended into heaven, two angels appeared with a message to His apostles:

> "Men of Galilee, why do you stand looking into heaven? This Jesus, who was taken up from you into heaven, will come in the same way as you saw him go into heaven." (Acts 1:11.)

The apostles took this promise to heart. Only two chapters later we find it reflected in Peter's public preaching:

> "Repent therefore, and turn again, that your sins may be blotted out, that times of refreshing may come from the presence of the Lord, and *that he may send the Christ appointed for you, Jesus, whom heaven must receive until the time for establishing all that God spoke by the mouth of his holy prophets from of old.*" (Acts 3:19–21.)

This is a particularly revealing passage. It not only tells us that God is going to send Jesus back to the earth. It also tells us why.

Jesus must come back to "establish all that God spoke by his holy prophets". In other words, He is coming to fulfil God's Old Testament promises.

Some of these promises go back a very long way. A

particularly reassuring one is found in Numbers, the fourth of the thirty-nine books in the Old Testament:

> "As truly as I live (said God) all the earth shall be filled with the glory of the Lord." (Num. 14:21, AV.)

So the earth is not going to end up as a lifeless ruin. Civilised Man is not going to be wiped out by famine and nuclear warfare, leaving a few wild-eyed survivors to return to barbarism. God has a better end in view. Somehow, He intends that this unhappy globe of ours will one day be filled with His glory.

As we go on through the Old Testament, promises of this kind multiply. Here are just a few of them; they are plain enough to speak for themselves.

HABAKKUK: "The earth will be filled with the knowledge of the glory of the Lord, as the waters cover the sea." (2:14.)

ZECHARIAH: "The Lord will become king over all the earth . . . He shall command peace to the nations; his dominion shall be from sea to sea, and from the River to the ends of the earth." (14:9 and 9:10.)

DANIEL: "In the days of those kings the God of heaven will set up a kingdom which shall never be destroyed, nor shall its sovereignty be left to another people. It shall break in pieces all these kingdoms and bring them to an end, and it shall stand for ever." (2:44.)

MICAH: "It shall come to pass in the latter days that the mountain of the house of the Lord shall be established as the highest of the mountains, and shall be raised up above the hills; and peoples shall flow to it, and many nations shall come, and say: 'Come, let us go up to the mountain of the Lord, to the house of the God of Jacob; that he may teach us his ways and we may walk in his paths.'

"For out of Zion shall go forth the law, and the word of the Lord from Jerusalem. He shall judge between many peoples, and shall decide for strong nations afar off; and they shall beat their swords into ploughshares and their spears into pruning hooks; nation shall not lift up sword against nation, neither shall they learn war any more; but they shall sit every man under his vine and under his fig tree, and none shall make them afraid." (4:1–4.)

Christianity in Retreat

A hundred years ago most Christians thought this state of affairs would come about gradually. They hoped that the gospel would spread throughout the whole world, changing the hearts of all men wherever it went.

Nowadays that idea has been quietly dropped. It can be seen as sheer wishful thinking. In any case, the Bible made it plain that the disciples' preaching would never have that much success: human nature would prove too great an obstacle. Consider these two sayings of Jesus:

> "When the Son of man comes, will he find faith on earth?" (Luke 18:8.)

> "Many will fall away, and betray one another, and hate one another. And many false prophets will arise and lead many astray. And because wickedness is multiplied, most men's love will grow cold. But he who endures to the end will be saved. And this gospel of the kingdom will be preached (not 'believed'; just 'preached') throughout the whole world as a testimony to all nations; and then the end will come . . . they will see the Son of man coming on the clouds of heaven with power and great glory." (Matt. 24:10–14, 30.)

Evidently Jesus expects to come back to a world that is in a bad way, a world that has largely rejected Christianity. A world, in fact, that is rather like the world we live in today.

When Jesus does at last return to a world in distress, what is He most likely to do? Go away again, and leave mankind to its own evil devices once more? Or take over the government of the world, and fulfil God's promise to fill this world with His glory?

Commonsense says that when Jesus comes He will want to stay and put the world right. So also does the Bible.

To begin with, the Lord Jesus Christ said so Himself. The nineteenth chapter of Luke records His "parable of the pounds". In it Christ likened Himself to a nobleman who "went into a far country to receive kingly power and then return". (v. 12.)

The Jews were quite familiar with the situation Jesus had described. Some of their puppet kings, like Archelaus, the son of the Herod who slew the babies in Bethlehem, had to go to Rome to have their authority confirmed by the emperor, before they could begin to rule.

"It is like that with me," said Jesus, in effect. "I must first go to see the Lord of heaven, and afterwards come back to earth to reign."

After the nobleman in the parable had "returned, having received his kingly power" he had two things to do. First, he called his own servants to see how they had served him in his absence. The faithful servants were given a reward; the worthless servants were punished. (Luke 19:15–26.)

This is an unmistakable picture of the Day of Judgment. On that occasion Chirst's flock will be sorted into sheep and goats (Matt. 25:31–46) the fish in the gospel net will be divided into edible and worthless fish (Matt. 13:47–50) the harvesters will sift out the wheat from the tares (Matt. 13:24–30)—to use the language of three other parables of the Judgment Day.

In plain language, Christ's first task when He returns will be to separate His would-be followers into two classes. The Peters and the Pauls and the Marthas and the Marys will be told, "Enter into the joy of your master." (Matt. 25:21.)

The others will be classed with the traitor Judas, the deceiver Ananias and his wife Sapphira. They will hear some of the most appalling words that have ever been uttered: "Cast the worthless servant into the outer darkness!" (Matt. 25:30.)

But all this is only a beginning. The nobleman comes back to the land of his birth with a title to a throne. His long-term work is to rule over his subjects, and the parable concludes with him starting to reign. (Luke 19:27.)

Jesus the Messiah

Jesus knew that He must return to govern the world because the Old Testament said so. And if a thing was written in the Scriptures, then, so far as Jesus was concerned, there was no room for argument. The following three remarks of His are typical of Christ's attitude to the Old Testament:

> "Think not that I have come to abolish the law and the prophets; I have come not to abolish them but to fulfil them. For truly, I say to you, till heaven and earth pass away, not an iota, not a dot, will pass from the law until all is accomplished." (Matt. 5:17, 18.)

> "Scripture cannot be broken." (John 10:35.)

> "*Everything* written about me in the law of Moses and the prophets and the psalms must be fulfilled." (Luke 24:44.)

With words like those to reassure us, we can turn back

confidently to the Old Testament. Everything it prophesied about Jesus will certainly be fulfilled. Jesus said so.

These Old Testament prophecies are usually called "Messianic prophecies", because they spoke of someone the Jews called *Messiah.*

This is a Hebrew word meaning "anointed". Israel's kings, priests and prophets were all anointed with oil when they first took office, just as British kings and queens are today in our coronation ceremony.

The Old Testament is full of promises about the coming of a divine man who would be a prophet, a priest and a king. He was given a number of different names in the Old Testament—The Rock, The Branch, Emmanuel, Messiah, and others. The Jews preferred the name Messiah, "The Anointed". It was a good name because it indicated what Messiah would have to do, and it stuck.

When the apostles preached to the Jews they declared that Jesus of Nazareth was the Messiah. The Greek word for "anointed" was *christos,* and so Jesus came to be known as "The Christ".

Many of the Old Testament prophecies about the coming Messiah have been fulfilled already.

For example, Isaiah said Messiah would be born miraculously, of a virgin mother (Isa. 7:14)—and Jesus was (Luke 1:26–31). Micah said Messiah would be born in the village of Bethlehem (Mic. 5:2)—and although this was far from the home of Joseph and Mary (Luke 2:4, 39) it still happened that way. (Matt. 2:1.) Isaiah said that Messiah would be sinless (Isa. 53:9) but despite this he would be executed as a criminal (Isa. 53:8)—and Jesus was (Luke 23:22–24).

David said that men would execute Messiah by piercing his hands and his feet (Ps. 22:26) and that his executioners would share his clothes between them (Ps. 22:18)—which they did. (Matt. 27:35.) In two other psalms David said that Messiah would rise from the dead (Ps. 16:9–11) and ascend to heaven (Ps. 110:1)—which Jesus did (Acts 3:15, 21).

There are many other Messianic prophecies that have not yet been fulfilled. They will be, one day; we can be sure of that. The fulfilment of so many prophecies when Jesus first came shows that God keeps His promises. When Jesus comes again the remaining prophecies about Him will come to pass.

These prophecies about the Second Coming are quite unlike the prophecies that were fulfilled when the Lord Jesus Christ first came. He will have a very different kind of work to do the second time He appears on earth. These other prophecies portray Messiah as an all-powerful and all-wise king, ruling over a worldwide kingdom of peaceful, joyous, righteous citizens. Here is a beautiful passage of this kind from Isaiah:

> "There shall come forth a shoot from the stump of Jesse, and a branch shall grow out of his roots. And the Spirit of the Lord shall rest upon him, the spirit of wisdom and understanding, the spirit of counsel and might, the spirit of knowledge and the fear of the Lord. And his delight shall be in the fear of the Lord.
>
> "He shall not judge by what his eyes see, or decide by what his ears hear; but with righteousness he shall judge the poor, and decide with equity for the meek of the earth; and he shall smite the earth with the rod of his mouth, and with the breath of his lips he shall slay the wicked. Righteousness shall be the girdle of his waist, and faithfulness the girdle of his loins.
>
> "The wolf shall dwell with the lamb, and the leopard shall lie down with the kid, and the calf and the lion and the fatling together, and a little child shall lead them . . . They shall not hurt or destroy in all my holy mountain; for the earth shall be full of the knowledge

of the Lord as the waters cover the sea." (Isa. 11:1–9.)

We know that this refers to Jesus, because the apostle Paul says so. (Rom. 15:12, which quotes Isa. 11:10.) Even without Paul's guidance we could hardly apply Isaiah's prophecy to anyone else. A ruler who is so filled with God's Spirit that His decisions are always right, a ruler who knows how to control the evil in mankind, a ruler who will succeed in filling the whole earth with peace, happiness and the glory of God—why, it reads almost like that job specification for a World President!

The King of the Jews

Jesus was on trial for His life. The charge: treason. He had claimed to be the Jews' Messiah (John 4:25, 26) and everybody knew what that meant. Messiah was going to be a mighty king, ruling first over Israel and then over the world. That made Jesus a rival to the Roman Emperor!

Pontius Pilate, the Emperor's representative, found it hard to take the accusation seriously. Jesus was more of a pacifist than a revolutionary. Pilate regarded Him as harmless, and said so. (Luke 23:1–4.)

But the mob was thirsting for blood. To avoid trouble Pilate was obliged to interrogate Jesus. "Are you the king of the Jews?" (John 18:33.)

"My kingship is not of this world," replied Jesus. "If my kingship were of this world, my servants would fight, that I might not be handed over to the Jews; but my kingship is not from the world." (John 18:36.)

In other words, "Well, yes, I am a king. But not your sort of a king. My kingly power does not depend on the swords of my followers."

Pilate evidently accepted what Jesus told him. When his cross-examination was finished he announced to the protesting Jews, "Here is your King!" (John 19:14.)

When he reluctantly gave in to their demands for a crucifixion Pilate insisted on having the last word. Despite the Jews' objections he wrote a signboard (John 19:19) and had it nailed to the cross:

"JESUS OF NAZARETH
THE KING OF THE JEWS"

The disciples of Jesus did not need to be told this. They had known all along. When the early disciple, Nathanael, was converted he delighted Jesus with this declaration of his belief: "Rabbi, you are the Son of God! You are the King of Israel!" (John 1:49.)

His mother Mary knew this, even before her son was born. An angel came to her as a young virgin, and explained the miracle that was about to take place in her womb. His message was based on an extract from the prophet Isaiah, and we can learn a great deal by comparing these two related passages of Scripture and seeing how closely they correspond. (See facing page.)

In those days Jewish girls knew their Old Testament very well indeed. As soon as the angel spoke, Mary's mind would have leapt to Isaiah. "He's quoting a Messianic prophecy!" she would have thought. "My son is going to be the Messiah, King of the Jews, ruler of the world, Lord of God's kingdom!"

When Mary died the angel's promise was still unfulfilled. With breaking heart she had seen the Jews crucify their king. She must have wondered, "When, oh, when is He going to reign over the house of Jacob (the Jews), as the angel said?"

His disciples certainly wondered about it. The very last thing they are recorded as saying to Him before He went to heaven was: "Lord, will you at this time restore the kingdom of Israel?" (Acts 1:6.)

He replied, "It is not for you to know times or seasons

ISAIAH'S PROPHECY: "(A) Unto us a child is born, unto us a son is given; and the government shall be upon his shoulder. (B) And his name shall be called Wonderful, Counsellor, The mighty God, The everlasting Father, The Prince of Peace. Of the increase of his government and peace there shall be (C) no end, upon (D) the throne of David, and upon (E) his kingdom." (Isa. 9:6, 7.)[2]	THE ANGEL'S WORDS TO MARY: "(A) Thou shalt conceive in thy womb and bring forth a son, and shalt call his name Jesus. (B) He shall be great and shall be called the Son of the Highest. And The Lord God shall give unto him (D) the throne of his father David; and he shall reign over the house of Jacob for ever, and of (E) his kingdom there shall be (C) no end." (Luke 1: 31–33.)[3]	The two sentences marked (A) speak of the birth of a son. The two (B)'s indicate that His "name" (which, to a Hebrew, meant His description) would be divine. Both (D)'s say that He would sit on David's throne—David being the great prototype of all the Jewish kings. The two (E)'s refer to His kingdom, and the (C)'s declare that it would have no end.

which the Father has fixed." (Acts 1:7.) As much as to say, "Just be patient. I shall do it when God is ready, but not before."

The King's Capital City

In one way this last conversation between Jesus and His disciples is puzzling. The gospel is for all nations. Christ's kingdom is to be a worldwide kingdom. Why, then, did they refer to it as an Israelitish kingdom?

The explanation is simple. Every kingdom needs a capital city; every ruler needs an administrative centre. And Jerusalem, in the land of Israel, will be Christ's headquarters when He rules over the world. He said so, in these words: "Jerusalem . . . is the city of the great King." (Matt. 5:35.)

Jesus did not think up that expression Himself. He

lifted it straight out of Psalm 48. There are lots of other Old Testament chapters He could have quoted—this one, for instance: "The Lord of hosts will reign on Mount Zion and in Jerusalem and before his elders he will manifest his glory." (Isa. 24:23.)

(Zion is the name of the hill on which the oldest part of Jerusalem was built.)

Jerusalem has several great advantages as a world capital. Look at a map of the world. Few other cities are as central as Jerusalem, which lies right in the middle of the world's greatest land mass, at the hub of three continents.

Then again, Jerusalem is the ideal capital because God intends to make special use of the Jews. Today they are an ungodly nation. But when Jesus comes they will be the first nation to experience a mass conversion. After that, God will use them to guide the other nations. As the prophet Zechariah says:

> "The inhabitants of one city shall go to another, saying, 'Let us go at once to entreat the favour of the Lord, and to seek the Lord of hosts; I am going.' Many peoples and strong nations shall come to seek the Lord of hosts in Jerusalem, and to entreat the favour of the Lord. Thus says the Lord of hosts: In those days ten men from the nations of every tongue shall take hold of the robe of a Jew, saying, 'Let us go with you, for we have heard that God is with you.' " (Zech. 8:21–23.)

Thy Kingdom Come

It is time to throw a spanner in the works. If I don't do it, some reader will. "This is all very well," he will say. "But Jesus is reigning in the hearts of all His followers already. The church is His world-wide kingdom. What need is there for any other kingdom?"

I can sympathise with this point of view. There is some truth in it. But it is not the whole truth.

Christ does indeed rule over those who follow Him today. His disciples are truly citizens of His kingdom. But they are citizens-in-exile, according to the apostle. (1 Pet. 2:11.) The world is not yet the kingdom of God and Christ. It is still a kingdom of Sin. Christ's disciples feel like foreigners in it, as He said they would. (John 15:18, 19.)

They long for this state of affairs to change. They want Christ's kingdom—their kingdom—to fill the earth. So every day they pray:

> "Thy kingdom come. Thy will be done in earth, as it is in heaven." Matt. 6:10, AV.)

They know they are praying for the second coming of their Lord. They know that when He comes a great trumpet will sound, and an angel will proclaim: "The kingdom of the world has become the kingdom of our Lord and of his Christ, and he shall reign for ever and ever." (Rev. 11:15.)

If God does not soon answer their prayers it looks as if it will be too late. Unless God intervenes the words of the unbeliever Bertrand Russell are bound to come true: "Over man and all his works, night falls pitiless and dark."

Thank God that He has made a promise. The man-made night is indeed about to fall. But it will soon end with the dawn of God's new day:

> "But for you who fear my name the sun of righteousness shall rise, with healing in its wings." (Mal. 4:2.)

Is this just wishful thinking, or are there really grounds for believing that Jesus will come soon?

In the next chapter we shall see.

5

THE JEWS AND THE GOOD NEWS

It had been a hard day's work in Jerusalem. Jesus had been preaching to great crowds in the Jewish temple. Now He and His disciples were going home to their lodgings on the Mount of Olives, a mile or so outside the city.

The Jews had been at work on this temple for some fifty years, and it was still far from complete. Another thirty-odd years were to elapse before the last stone was put in place. But already the temple was one of the world's finest buildings, with its outer porches of pillared marble enclosing an area more than a thousand feet square.

As they were leaving the unfinished building the disciples pointed out some of its superb features to Jesus. They were used to getting surprises from their Master, but this time His answer really stunned them: "You see all these, do you not? Truly, I say to you, there will not be left here one stone upon another, that will not be thrown down." (Matt. 24:2.)

This magnificent building to be destroyed? Why, it was Israel's pride and joy. What a horrible prospect! As soon as they had the Master to Himself upon the Mount of Olives, they asked Him to explain Himself:

"Tell us, (1) when will this be, and (2) what will be the sign of your coming and of the close of the age?" (Matt. 24:3.)

This was such an important question that Matthew, Mark and Luke all devoted a long chapter to the answer. The first part of Christ's explanation is now ancient history. The temple was utterly destroyed by the Romans in A.D. 70—only six years after it was completed.

The second part of the Lord's reply is still a red hot issue. Sincere Christians today are just as anxious as the apostles to know "what will be the sign of His coming and of the close of the age". This is an extract from Christ's answer, with some comments upon it:

"(A) But when you see Jerusalem surrounded by armies, then know that its desolation has come near. (B) Then let those who are in Judea flee to the mountains, and let those who are inside the city depart, and let not those who are out in the country enter it; for these are days of vengeance, (C) to fulfil all that is written.

"Alas for those who are with child and for those who give suck in those days! (D) For great distress shall be upon the earth and wrath upon this people; they will fall by the edge of the sword, (E) and be led captive among all nations; (F) and Jerusalem will be trodden down by the Gentiles, until the times of the Gentiles are fulfilled." (Luke 21: 20–24.)

(A) This happened in A.D. 67, when the Romans besieged Jerusalem after the Jews there had rebelled.

(B) When the Roman armies encircled Jerusalem they looked as if they were about to capture it. Then, for some unexplained reason, they temporarily withdrew. The Christians of Jerusalem took their Lord's advice and seized their brief opportunity to escape, before the Roman siege began in real earnest.

A Jewish historian told how they fled to safety in the mountains of Perea. By accepting the truth of Christ's prophecy they saved their lives. (There is a lesson here, if we like to learn it.)

(C) Jesus obviously meant, "all that is written *in the Old Testament*". All the prophecies of the Old Testament are bound to be fulfilled, according to this statement and an even more emphatic one in Luke 24: 44. Many were fulfilled during His first coming. Some have been fulfilled since. Lots of others will have their thrilling fulfilment when He comes again.

(D) "Great distress" was right. The Jewish-Roman war of A.D. 66–70—and especiallly its climax, the siege of Jerusalem—was one of the most frightful bloodbaths in all history.

(E) This also was fulfilled literally. Slave-markets all over the Roman world were glutted with Jewish captives.

(F) See foot of next page.

The Jew, God's Signpost

The Jewish nation features very prominently in this speech made by the Lord Jesus. That is only what we might expect. The Bible is a Jewish book. Jesus Himself was a Jew. The twelve apostles were Jews. So were practically all the very early converts to Christianity.

The Jews occupy a great place in the purpose of God. In fact, the whole history of mankind, both past and future, revolves around the history of Israel. When Jesus was on earth before, He said, "Salvation is from the Jews." (John 4:22.) When He is here again, there will be a great work for the Jews to do. One prophet says this about Israel:

> "For Zion's sake will I (God) not hold my peace, and for Jerusalem's sake I will not rest, until the righteousness thereof go forth as brightness . . . And the Gentiles shall see thy righteousness, and all kings thy glory." (Isa. 62:1, 2, AV.)

> "Ye shall be named the priests of the Lord; men shall call you the ministers of our God . . . Their seed shall be known among the Gentiles, and their offspring among the people." (Isa. 61:6, 9, AV.)

Isaiah was obviously referring to the place of Israel in Christ's kingdom, after His return to earth. At present the Jews—just like every other race—are much more

---

(F) So was this, although not at once. After its destruction in A.D. 70 the Jews rebuilt Jerusalem, and in A.D. 132 they again fought the Romans for their independence. In A.D. 135 the Romans counter-attacked, and Israel suffered another crushing defeat.

This time the Romans banished all Jews from Judea, the heart of their country. Jerusalem was turned into a Roman city with a Roman name, Aelia Capitolina, and a Roman temple of Jupiter. For the next eighteen centuries Jerusalem was to be "trodden down of the Gentiles", just as Jesus had prophesied.

interested in serving themselves than in serving God.

But even today the Jews are fulfilling a purpose. Without even realising it they are acting as God's signpost to the world. For those who have eyes to see, Israel shows just where we stand in relation to the Second Coming.

To appreciate this we need to go back to the early days of Israel's history. Shortly after they received the Law from Mount Sinai, God gave His people a solemn warning:

> "If in spite of this you will not hearken to me, but walk contrary to me, then . . . I will lay your cities waste, and will make your sanctuaries desolate, and I will not smell your pleasing odours. And I will devastate the land, so that your enemies who settle in it shall be astonished at it. And I will scatter you among the nations . . ." (Lev. 26:27–33.)

This prophecy was written down by Moses, well over a thousand years before the time of Christ. Yet it bears a striking resemblance to the words of Christ quoted above. Like Jesus, Moses prophesied the devastation of the Jews' homeland and its occupation by foreigners. Like Jesus, he foretold the long period of Jewish exile, "scattered among the nations".

In Deuteronomy 28 Moses enlarged upon his earlier prophecy. He made it clear that the Israelites in exile would have a miserable time. They would be despised and cruelly persecuted. They would flee from one country to another in search of lasting peace, and never find it. These are his words:

> "You shall become a horror, a proverb, and a byword, among all the peoples where the Lord will lead you away . . . You shall be plucked off the land which you are entering to take possession of it. And the Lord

will scatter you among all peoples, from one end of the earth to the other . . .

"And among these nations you shall find no ease, and there shall be no rest for the sole of your foot; but the Lord will give you there a trembling heart, and failing eyes, and a languishing soul; your life shall hang in doubt before you; night and day you shall be in dread, and have no assurance of your life. In the morning you shall say, 'Would it were evening!' and at evening you shall say, 'Would it were morning!' because of the dread which your heart shall fear, and the sights which your eyes shall see." (Deut. 28:37, 63–67.)

The World's Best-Hated Nation

For many centuries these grim words were continuously fulfilled. Always unpopular, always unwanted, the Jews lived out their unhappy lives. Yet with all the odds seeming to be against them, the Jews somehow managed to survive.

But of course, they were bound to survive. God had promised that they would not perish. It would be a miracle if they did survive—but God declared that this miracle would take place:

"I am with you (Israel) to save you, says the Lord; I will make a full end of all the nations among whom I scattered you, but *of you I will not make a full end.*" (Jer. 30:11.)

"For lo, I will command,
And shake the house of Israel among all the nations
As one shakes with a sieve,
But *no pebble shall fall upon the earth.*" (Amos 9:9.)

The vivid poetry of Amos supports the plain prose of Jeremiah. Remember the last time you watched a gardener shaking a sieve? The stones jerk up and down, to and fro, as if in agony. But although the soil drops through the holes to lose its identity in the heap beneath, the pebbles never fall through.

"It will be like that with Israel", was the evident message of Amos. "They will be tossed to and fro across Europe, Asia and North Africa. But they will never disappear into the great mass of mankind. God will preserve them intact, through all their sufferings." And so God did.

The prophets gave Israel a second message of consolation. The nation's troubles would not last for ever. One day, after a long, long time, the children of Israel would be brought back to their God:

> "The children of Israel shall dwell many days without king or prince, without sacrifice or pillar, without ephod or teraphim. *Afterward the children of Israel shall return and seek the Lord their God,* and David their king; and they shall come in fear to the Lord and to his goodness in the latter days." (Hos. 3:4, 5.)

Israel Today

This brings us back to the words of the Lord Jesus upon the Mount of Olives. He told His disciples that all these Old Testament prophecies about Israel were going to be fulfilled. He mentioned especially the fall of Jerusalem and the destruction of its temple, the scattering of the Jews throughout the world, and the Gentile occupation of their land. "Jerusalem", He said, "will be trodden down by the Gentiles, until the times of the Gentiles are fulfilled." (Luke 21:24.)

In these words Jesus was probably referring to a passage in Isaiah, where the prophet says to Jerusalem:

> "You have made your back like the ground and like

the street for them to pass over. Awake, awake, put on your strength, O Zion; put on your beautiful garments, O Jerusalem, the holy city; for there shall no more come into you the uncircumcised (Gentiles) and unclean." (Isa. 51:23–52:1.)

Isaiah and Jesus both indicate that Jerusalem would not be "trodden down by the Gentiles" for ever, but only "until the times of the Gentiles are fulfilled". Isaiah goes on to connect the recovery of Jerusalem with the coming of the kingdom of God. Similarly, Jesus links it with His second coming. Three verses later on He says:

> "And then they will see the Son of man coming in a cloud with power and great glory. *Now when these things begin to take place, look up and raise your heads, because your redemption is drawing near.*" (Luke 21:27, 28.)

The words printed in italics are a command. Christians have a duty to recognise the indications that Christ's return is near. When they see those signs, they are commanded to "look up and raise their heads". Instead of being gloomy because the world is in such a mess, they are to rejoice in the evidence that their Master is at hand. And of all the signs of His nearness, the most unmistakable is the restoration of Israel.

The facts speak for themselves. In 1800 there were only a few thousand Jews in the entire Holy Land, out of a worldwide Jewish population of several million. In 1900 there were still only a few tens of thousands.

By 1948, when the independent state of Israel was born, its Jewish population had zoomed up to six hundred thousand. A little over ten years later it topped the two million mark.

Nearly every aspect of Israel's development is

breath-taking. Today Tel Aviv is among the world's great commercial cities. Yet its older inhabitants can remember the day when its site was just a heap of sandhills in a hostile land.

Jerusalem's story is still more striking. On 4th June, 1967, it was an Arab city belonging to Jordan. The next morning Israeli jets attacked Egyptian airfields and the Six-Day War was on. Within a week the Israeli flag flew over Mount Zion.

For the first time in eighteen centuries, Jerusalem was a Jewish city.

At long last, it was no longer "trodden down by the Gentiles".

Israel the Stony-hearted

This means that the Second Coming cannot be far away. We are right in the period called by the prophets, "the latter (last) days", or, "the time of the end".

But it does not necessarily mean that Jerusalem will never be recaptured by the Arabs. Many prophecies tell us that terrible things will happen in the Holy Land in the latter days. The young nation of Israel is due to suffer at least one big defeat before the Lord returns—a defeat infinitely greater than the minor setback of the 1973 war. (See Zech. 14:1–4; Joel 3:1, 2; Dan. 11:40, 41.)

Nor does it mean that there is anything admirable about the Israelis' behaviour. By and large they are a self-seeking, arrogant, godless people. Almost to a man they do not believe in Jesus Christ. What is perhaps worse is that a very large number of Israelis, including many of their leaders, do not even believe in God.

But this is only to be expected. It is exactly what Ezekiel prophesied about Israel. He said they would be an ungodly nation in their exile, and an ungodly nation when they first went back home in the last days:

"The word of the Lord came to me: 'Son of man, when the house of Israel dwelt in their own land, they defiled it by their ways and their doings. So I poured out my wrath upon them ... I scattered them among the nations, and they were dispersed through the countries ... But when they came to the nations, wherever they came, they profaned my holy name ...

" 'Therefore say to the house of Israel, Thus says the Lord God: *It is not for your sake*, O house of Israel, that I am about to act, but for the sake of my holy name, which you have profaned among the nations ... For I will take you from the nations, and gather you from all the countries, and bring you into your own land. I will sprinkle clean water upon you, and you shall be clean from all your uncleannesses, and from all your idols I will cleanse you.

" 'A new heart I will give you, and a new spirit I will put within you; and I will take out of your flesh the heart of stone and give you a heart of flesh. And I will put my spirit within you and cause you to walk in my statutes.' " (Ezek. 36:16–27.)

In his next chapter the prophet repeated this message with the aid of a parable. He described a valley filled with human bones. God declared that He would bring those bones back to life.

In response to His command the isolated bones sorted themselves out and joined up to form complete skeletons. Then sinews appeared on the bones. Then they became padded out with flesh. Finally, skin covered them over. At that stage the valley was filled with human bodies, fully formed but lifeless.

Then God put the breath of life into them, and "they lived, and stood upon their feet, an exceedingly great host". (Ezek. 37:10.)

Ezekiel goes on to explain the parable. The collection of

dried bones is the Jewish people. As a nation they are as good as dead, helpless and hopeless. Therefore God will work a miracle. He will recreate His nation in their own land.

But even after their regathering there is still one sense in which they are a dead nation. So the story ends with God putting His Spirit into their dead bodies, and at last they come alive.

A Change of Heart

This parable describes the present condition of Israel perfectly. God has wrought a tremendous miracle with His people. It has been like a national resurrection from the dead. Despite the fierce opposition of a hundred million Arabs, the nation has been reborn.

Yet that virile young nation is still dead—spiritually. The majority of its inhabitants are thoroughgoing materialists. There is a substantial religious minority, but most of its members are steeped in the traditions of the Pharisees.

Just as Ezekiel prophesied, twentieth-century Israelis need a reformation. They need the Spirit of God to give them life. They need their Messiah, to "take away their heart of stone, and give them a heart of flesh".

Another prophet tells us precisely how this change of heart will come about:

> "I (God) will pour out on the house of David and the inhabitants of Jerusalem a spirit of compassion and supplication so that, *when they look on him whom they have pierced,* they shall mourn for him, as one mourns for an only child, and weep bitterly over him . . .
>
> "On that day there shall be a fountain opened for the house of David and the inhabitants of Jerusalem to cleanse them from sin and uncleanness." (Zech. 12:10 and 13:1.)

The children of Israel will have waited more than three thousand years for their Messiah. When at last He does appear, they will be utterly shattered. He will be a man with the marks of crucifixion in His body—the man whose execution their forefathers approved, and whom they have always rejected!

Brokenhearted Israel will weep bitter tears of shame. But their God will wipe away their tears, and wash away their sin. At last they will own Jesus as their Lord and their Saviour. At long last God will be able to use them as ministers of His Word, as examples to all the other nations in His kingdom.

Grounds for Belief

God always gives His people good grounds for belief.

More than three thousand years ago He led Israel through the Red Sea. He displayed His power to them on Sinai and worked miracle after miracle through Moses, so that they might believe. But most of them didn't.

Nearly two thousand years ago He raised Jesus from the dead, and gave the Holy Spirit to His disciples. You might have thought that with signs like this the Jews would have accepted their Saviour. Yet the great majority didn't.

Today God gives equally strong proof that the Second Coming is near. It must be recognised that some prophecies in the Bible are obscurely worded. Such prophecies are difficult to understand, and they may need interpretation. *But the prophecies quoted above about Israel are not like this.*

They are plainly worded. Their message cannot be misunderstood. They foretold the scattering of the Jews, their long exile, and their eventual return home in a condition of unbelief. And this, said Jesus and the prophets, would be a prelude to the coming of their Messiah.

All this (except the very last step) has come true, with

uncanny precision. No atheist can explain away these facts. The restoration of Israel that Jesus foretold has happened once, and once only. It cannot be confused with any other event in history.

It is the sign that God has given His people—the unique, unmistakable, undeniable, sign—that the Lord Jesus Christ will return to this earth in our time.

With such clear evidence you might have thought that most men would believe in the Second Coming. Yet most men don't. Unfortunately, we need not be surprised by their unbelief.

Human nature has always been like that.

6

WHY THE WORLD WON'T BE DESTROYED

"Heard the news? An atomic bomb has been dropped on Hiroshima, and has wiped out the whole city!"

It was 6th August, 1945. I was one of a group of young people who were spending their summer holidays in Aberdeen, helping with a Back-to-the-Bible campaign.

For a few moments there was a hush. Eventually one young man muttered under his breath, "Them that destroy the earth."

"What are you on about, Larry?" we asked him.

"I was thinking of a verse in the Book of Revelation," he replied. "It's been on my mind for a long time. It never made sense to me before—or to anyone else, I imagine. But now it's obvious what it means.

"It says that when Jesus comes back, He will '*destroy them which destroy the earth.*' " (Rev. 11:18, AV.)

"Now that men have unlocked the power of the atom, they will be able, for the first time in history, to destroy the earth if they choose. And the Bible foresaw this!"

Since that time it has become clear that several other aspects of our twentieth-century crisis were foreseen in the Bible, too. The Lord Jesus Christ referred to some of them Himself.

In the previous chapter we looked at a part of His famous prophecy uttered on the Mount of Olives. In that chapter we were only concerned with the Jewish sign that His second coming is near. Consequently, we jumped from Luke 21:24—"Jerusalem will be trodden down by the Gentiles, until the times of the Gentiles are fulfilled", to verse 27—"And then they will see the Son of man coming in a cloud with power and great glory."

Now we must go back and look at the two verses we skipped over, which describe the state of the Gentile world just before Christ returns. They tell us:

> "And there will be signs in sun and moon and stars, and upon the earth distress of nations in perplexity at the roaring of the sea and the waves, men fainting with fear and with foreboding of what is coming on the world; for the powers of the heavens will be shaken." (Luke 21:25, 26.)

These words were easier for Christ's Jewish listeners to understand than for us. The Jews frequently used the terms, "heaven", "sun, moon and stars", "sea and waves", in a figurative sense. Several Old Testament writers use the heavens and the heavenly bodies as symbols of ruling powers, and the earth and the sea as symbols of the common people.

Isaiah, for example, uses language very like that of Jesus. When the rulers of Babylon were overthrown, this was a catastrophe "in heaven", with the "sun, moon and stars" being darkened. (Isa. 13:5–13.) Turmoil among the nations of the world was "like the thundering of the sea . . . the roaring of mighty waters". (Isa. 17:12.)

Whether we take these expressions literally or figuratively, however, is of little consequence. The remainder of Christ's words are plain enough. "Distress of nations in perplexity", and "men fainting with fear and with foreboding at what is coming on the world" are a perfect description of our tormented world. We can all see what is coming, but we can't see how to avert it.

And that, says Jesus, is the state the world will be in when He comes again! That is why He is coming back—to "destroy them which destroy the earth".

There may perhaps be a reference to the H-bomb in Christ's last phrase, "the powers of the heavens will be shaken". It is a fact that the principle of the H-bomb was discovered by astronomers studying the sun. The sun's fierce heat is produced by the conversion of hydrogen into helium. When they discovered how to reproduce this process on earth, scientists were able to build the first hydrogen bomb.

As Professors Ward and Dubos have said: "To generate this power on earth is, almost literally, the Promethean act of stealing fire from the gods ... This technique is, literally, the transfer to earth of the sun's processes."[1]

By their fiendish ingenuity men are now able to create miniature suns on earth, for use as weapons. They have learnt to exploit "the powers of the heavens"!

Modern Warfare is Warfire

The coming of the A-bomb and H-bomb solved another long-standing problem for Bible students.

Many prophecies in the Bible speak of the time of the Second Coming as a time of judgment, when an evil world will receive the punishment it deserves. But they differ in their teaching about the nature of the punishment. Some passages say that it will be worldwide war; others speak of fire.

Here is a selection of these passages. They are not phrases taken out of context just to support a theory. In every case the Biblical author is actually speaking of the coming of Messiah (Old Testament) or Jesus (New Testament).

(A) "they ... go abroad to *the kings of the whole world, to assemble them for battle* on the great day of God the Almighty. ('Lo, I am coming like a thief! [says Jesus] Blessed is he who is awake, keeping his garments that he may not go naked and be seen exposed!') And they assembled them at the place which is called in Hebrew Armageddon." (Rev. 16:14–16.)

(B) "For behold, in those days and at that time, when I restore the fortunes of Judah and Jerusalem, *I will gather all the nations* and bring them down to the valley of Jehoshaphat, and I will enter into judgment with them there . . . Proclaim this among the nations: *Prepare war,* stir up the mighty men . . . Multitudes, multitudes, in the valley of decision! For the day of the Lord is near in the valley of decision.

"The sun and the moon are darkened, and the stars withdraw their shining. And the Lord roars from Zion, and utters His voice from Jerusalem, and the heavens and the earth shake." (Joel 3:1–16.)

(C) "Behold a day of the Lord is coming when the spoil taken from you will be divided in the midst of you. For *I will gather all the nations against Jerusalem to battle,* and the city shall be taken . . . Then the Lord will go forth and fight against those nations . . . On that day his feet shall stand on the Mount of Olives." (Zech. 14:1–4.)

(D) "Behold, the Lord will lay waste the earth and make it desolate, and he will twist its surface and scatter its inhabitants. . . . The earth lies polluted under its inhabitants; for they have transgressed the laws, violated the statutes, broken the everlasting covenant . . . therefore *the inhabitants of the earth are scorched, and few men are left* . . .

"Then the moon will be confounded, and the sun ashamed; for the Lord of hosts will reign on Mount Zion and in Jerusalem and before his elders he will manifest his glory." (Isa. 24:1, 5, 6, 23.)

(E) "Scoffers will come in the last days with scoffing,

following their own passions and saying, 'Where is the promise of his coming? For ever since the fathers fell asleep, all things have continued as they were from the beginning of creation . . .'

"The Lord is not slow about his promise as some count slowness, but is forbearing . . . But the day of the Lord will come like a thief, and then the heavens will pass away with a loud noise, and *the elements will be dissolved with fire, and the earth and the works that are upon it will be burned up.*" (2 Pet. 3:3, 4, 9, 10.)

Now glance back over those five Scriptures, and take note of the following points:

(1) All five are speaking of "the day of the Lord", when God will intervene forcefully in world affairs.

(2) The references to the "sun, moon and stars" in (B) and (D), and to "the heavens" in (B) and (E), are very reminiscent of the words of Jesus on the Mount of Olives. Like His use of the same expressions these are probably figures of speech, referring to the present ruling classes of the nations. They will be "eclipsed" by Jesus, in having to hand over their power to Him when He comes.

(3) The last sentence of the Old Testament passage (C) ties up marvellously with a passage in the New Testament. It was from the Mount of Olives that Jesus ascended into heaven. It was on this very mountain that the angels announced, "This Jesus, who was taken up from you into heaven, will come in the same way as you saw him go into heaven." (Acts 1:11.) If He is to come again "in the same way" as He went, we should expect Him to set foot first upon the Mount of Olives. And this, said Zechariah, is exactly what He will do.

(4) These things happen, according to (B), "at that time when I (God) restore the fortunes of Judah and Jerusalem". This links together the Jewish sign of the previous chapter with the Gentile signs of this chapter.

(5) Above all, look at the words in italics. (A), (B) and (C) speak of world *war*; (D) and (E) refer to worldwide judgments of *fire*.

When the Bible was first written there was no way to harmonise these statements. It must have looked like a glaring contradiction. In those days war was waged with iron blades and armour, whilst giant catapults were the ultimate weapon. Fire was not a weapon of war, to be employed against people. Its only use was to destroy captured cities after their inhabitants had been killed or had fled.

In recent years fire has been used as a weapon to an ever increasing extent. Think of incendiary bombs, flame-throwers, napalm, and finally, The Bomb. When World War III comes, who can doubt that the words of (D) and (E) will be fulfilled?

Mystery Plague

Another verse that baffled Bible students for centuries was Zechariah 14:12. This described a strange pestilence that would afflict the soldiers fighting in Armageddon:

> "And this shall be the plague with which the Lord will smite all the peoples that wage war against Jerusalem (in the last days): their flesh shall rot while they are still on their feet, their eyes shall rot in their sockets, and their tongues shall rot in their mouths."

What does it all mean? Until recent years no one could guess.

Sir Risdon Bennett was one of England's greatest doctors in his day. His book, *The Diseases of the Bible,*[2] is a classic of its kind. He analysed every disease referred to in Scripture, and put a name to it.

But when he came to Zechariah 14:12 this top expert gave up. He was like the ancient traveller confronting his first giraffe, "Coo, there ain't no such thing!" The best he could offer was the very long shot, "May it be intended to describe an army dying of famine?"

Nowadays there are two reasonable explanations of the verse. Both are equally spine-chilling.

The more obvious possibility is that these words might relate to chemical or biological warfare. Perhaps they make more sense to the hush-hush gentlemen in Her Majesty's most secret laboratories at Porton, than to the man in the street.

But it is equally possible that they are connected with atomic warfare. In 1945 John Hersey interviewed a number of people who survived the bomb on Hiroshima, and their accounts make fascinating though gruesome reading. Here are two of them:

> "Mr. Tanimoto ... reached down and took a woman by the hands, but her skin slipped off in huge glove-like pieces ... he remembered uneasily what the great burns he had seen during the day had been like: yellow at first, then red and swollen, with the skin sloughed off."[3]

(Compare Zechariah: "Their flesh shall rot while they are still on their feet.")

> "When he (Father Kleinsorge) had penetrated the bushes, he saw there were about twenty men, and they were all in exactly the same nightmarish state: their faces were wholly burned, their eyesockets were hollow, the fluid from their melted eyes had run down their cheeks."[4]

(Compare Zechariah: "Their eyes shall rot in their sockets.")

> "There shall be a time of trouble, such as never has been since there was a nation till that time; but at that time your people shall be delivered, every one whose name shall be found written in the book." (Dan. 12:1.)

We don't need to guess what period the prophet is speaking about. In the next verse he describes the Resurrection and the Day of Judgment. Consequently, it is clear that Daniel's great "time of trouble" occurs in the last days—the period in which we now live.

Jesus borrowed this saying from the prophet Daniel, and incorporated it in His own Mount of Olives prophecy:

> "There will be great tribulation, such as has not been from the beginning of the world until now, no, and never will be. And if those days had not been shortened, no human being would be saved; but for the sake of the elect those days will be shortened." (Matt. 24:21, 22. Also, Mark 13:19, 20.)

These verses introduce us to a very interesting feature of Bible prophecy. When we first read these words in their context it is difficult to decide how to apply them. The verses just before seem to link them with the Jewish disaster of A.D. 70. Yet the words that follow evidently relate them to the world disaster of the last days.

There is a simple explanation for this. God's character always stays the same, and human nature does not change much, either. Consequently history—especially the history of God's dealings with Man—repeats itself.

For this reason many Bible prophecies have a double fulfilment. This is one of them. It is at one and the same time a prophecy of both the great disasters mentioned above. It had a preliminary or partial fulfilment when the Romans massacred the Jews in A.D. 70. But the complete fulfilment is still ahead of us, although it is coming closer every day.

The coming of this "time of trouble such as never has been" is one of the best-known aspects of Bible prophecy. It is usually called, "the tribulation", after the word that Jesus used.

Unfortunately this phrase "the tribulation" is frequently given a narrower meaning than it deserves. Many people use it to denote a brief period, right at the end of the latter days, when an evil dictator known as "Antichrist", or "the man of sin" gains momentary control of the world. It is generally thought that God's people will be taken away to meet Christ when Antichrist arises.

Now up to a point these ideas are sound. It is certainly true that there will be a "rapture" of all Christ's true followers. ("Rapture" means "a snatching away", from the Latin word *raptus*.) As Paul said:

> "The Lord himself will descend from heaven ... And the dead in Christ will rise first; then we who are alive, who are left, shall be caught up together with them in the clouds to meet the Lord in the air; and so we shall always be with the Lord." (1 Thess. 4:16, 17.)

It is also probably true that, as our poor world slides into chaos, an evil dictator will seize power before he is finally crushed by Christ. Several prophecies in Daniel and Revelation seem to teach this. But they are highly symbolic prophecies. They need patient study and interpretation, and expositors have reached widely differing conclusions about them.

When the time comes we shall see which of these many earnest expositors was closest to the mark. Meanwhile, if we are wise, we shall try to avoid holding dogmatic views about doubtful details. As the scientist Sir Isaac Newton (a great student of Bible prophecy) said, "Let time be the interpreter."

In any case, *the tribulation period is not confined to the brief reign of the man of sin.*

His reign is only one aspect of the coming world catastrophe. The tribulation that Jesus spoke of includes *all* the horrors that unregenerate man is going to bring upon himself: overpopulation, pollution, starvation, civil disorder, revolution, persecution, chemical, biological and atomic warfare—you name it.

We have seen in the earlier chapters of this book that all these dreadful things are already on the horizon. Now the evidence is piling up that the Bible has foretold these terrible events. As always, the Bible is the answer to the world's need. It promises that Jesus will come in time to prevent Man destroying himself.

Beware Wishful Thinking

There is a popular idea that the rapture will take place before the tribulation begins. Many people hold this idea because it is pleasant. They like to think that they will not have to suffer, and so they cling to the belief that Christians wil be taken away before the latter-day troubles can affect them.

Unfortunately this notion is another half-truth. It is true that God will deliver His people from ultimate destruction, and give them immortality to enjoy in His everlasting kingdom. God's final judgments are to fall upon a wicked world, not upon His own faithful servants. They will be taken away before God's wrath descends directly on mankind.

But God's people cannot expect to escape all the tribulations of the latter days. These will extend over a period.

In the early stages there will be no need for God to act. He only needs to stand back and allow mankind to reap the consequences of its own sin and folly. Man will bring the tribulation upon himself at first. Only at the end, when human nature rises up in open rebellion against its Maker, will the tribulation conclude with a more direct outpouring of divine judgment.

It is sheer wishful thinking to believe that God will deliver His own children from all the early, man-made, stages of the tribulation. God does not promise us this.

On the contrary, Jesus said, "For the sake of the elect those days (of tribulation) will be shortened." (Matt. 24:22.) This implies that "the elect" (that is to say, true Christians) will have to endure at least the first part of the tribulation.

There is a historical parallel in the case of the "Jewish tribulation", to which Jesus also referred in His Mount of Olives prophecy, as we saw in the previous chapter. The early Christians in Jerusalem had to go through the first part of the Jewish-Roman war before God opened up a way of escape for them.

Moreover, in that same prophecy Jesus spoke words to His first-century disciples that almost certainly apply in the twentieth century also:

> "And you will hear of wars and rumours of wars; see that you are not alarmed; for this must take place, but the end is not yet. For nation will rise against nation, and kingdom against kingdom, and there will be famines and earthquakes in various places: all this is but the beginning of the suffering.
>
> "Then they will deliver you up to tribulation, and put you to death; and you will be hated by all nations for my name's sake . . . *But he who endures to the end will be saved.*" (Matt. 24:6–13.)

Evidently the world will need its full quota of faithful disciples as it enters into its last great tribulation. They will have work to do for their Master. As long as there is still time for men to repent and turn to Jesus, His servants will have to stay and preach His gospel.

It will not be easy for them. But they and their eleventh-hour converts will have every incentive to "endure to the end" (of the first stage of the tribulation). He who does so "will be saved".

The Moral Landslide

The statistics speak for themselves. Drink, drugs, crime, sex—all the graphs are shooting off the top of the page. Every year society becomes a bit more permissive than the year before.

Fortunately we need not be depressed about it. This is one more sign that Christ's coming is close at hand. He said so Himself:

> "As it was in the days of Noah, so will it be in the days of the Son of man. They ate, they drank, they married, they were given in marriage, until the day when Noah entered the ark, and the flood came and destroyed them all.
>
> "Likewise as it was in the days of Lot—they ate, they drank, they bought, they sold, they planted, they built, but on the day when Lot went out from Sodom fire and brimstone rained from heaven and destroyed them all—so will it be on the day when the Son of man is revealed." (Luke 17:26–30.)

Thus Christ foretold that the world in the last days would be like Sodom in the time of Lot, and like the world in the days of Noah.

Everyone knows what Sodom was famous for: immorality. Our permissive society is steadily transforming

Christendom into the latter-day Sodom that Christ foresaw.

Yet for some reason Jesus stressed the materialism of the Sodomites, rather than their permissiveness: "They ate, they drank, they bought, they sold, they planted, they built."

In a moment we shall see the reason for this. Meanwhile it is enough to note that Christ's comment agreed with the Old Testament. Sodom was an exceptionally prosperous place. That was why Lot chose to live there:

> "Lot lifted up his eyes, and saw that the Jordan valley was well watered everywhere like the garden of the Lord . . . So Lot chose for himself all the Jordan valley . . . Lot dwelt among the cities of the valley and moved his tent as far as Sodom." (Gen. 13:10–12.)

Turning to the world that Noah knew, we find a rather different picture. Jesus again emphasises its materialism, but the Old Testament begins the story of Noah like this:

> "(A) When men began to multiply on the face of the ground, and daughters were born to them, (B) the sons of God saw that the daughters of men were fair; and they took to wife such of them as they chose . . . the earth was corrupt in God's sight, and (C) the earth was filled with violence." (Gen. 6:1, 2, 11.)

A very familiar picture is painted in (A). As *The Living Bible* translates this phrase, "Now a population explosion took place upon the earth."

In (B) we have the old story of permissiveness and corruption. And (C) presents another modern phenomenon: a world filled with violence.

We can therefore summarise the Bible's descriptions of Noah's world and Lot's home town like this:

NOAH'S DAY AND AGE	LOT'S DAY AND AGE
Materialism	Materialism
Immorality	Immorality
Population Explosion	
	Prosperity
Universal Violence	

When we add the two lists together, it is obvious why Jesus likens the last days to the days of Noah and of Lot.

Our day and age bears an astonishing resemblance to the time of Noah and the time of Lot, combined into one!

Once again the facts speak for themselves. The Bible clearly foresaw the age in which we live. Our time is the most exciting period in world history—the period when the Son of God is coming back to rule the world.

The Knowledge Explosion

One more sign that the Second Coming is near remains to be considered. The prophet Daniel wrote:

> "You, Daniel, shut up the words, and seal the book, until the time of the end. Many shall run to and fro, and knowledge shall increase." (Dan. 12:4.)

At first glance the meaning of this seems obvious. Two notable things were to happen at the time of the end. First, there was to be a lot of "running to and fro". And secondly, knowledge would increase.

Many a preacher has enthralled his congregation with accounts of the marvels of modern transport, and of the way in which the sum total of human knowledge is doubling every ten or twenty years. Yes, at a quick glance this does seem to be a remarkable fulfilment of Daniel's words.

But first glances at the Bible often lead to wrong conclusions. Very often, the truth only emerges when you take a second, longer, more careful look.

The first rule of sound Bible study is this: *let the Bible interpret itself.* One passage of Scripture very often throws a flood of light on another passage.

So it is in this case. The prophet Amos lived about two centuries before the time of Daniel. His prophecy was part of Daniel's Bible—the inspired library that Daniel called, "The Books". (Dan. 9:2.) And Amos had foretold the period of Israel's unbelief in words that help us to see what Daniel evidently meant:

> "Behold, the days are coming, says the Lord God, when I will send a famine on the land (of Israel); not a famine of bread, nor a thirst for water, but of hearing the words of the Lord. They shall wander from sea to sea, and from north to east: *they shall run to and fro, to seek the word of the Lord,* but they shall not find it." (Amos 8:11,12.)

Daniel's prophecy shows that he knew his Bible very well indeed. He must have been well aware that, in Amos, "running to and fro" referred to strenuous—though unsuccessful—activity in pursuit of God's Word.

Consequently, it seems most likely that the "running to and fro" of the last days means increased activity by Bible students. And similarly, the knowledge that Daniel said would "be increased" evidently means the knowledge of God's Word.

Now look back at what Daniel himself was told by God. He was to "shut up the words and seal the book until the time of the end". Since he was addressed by name it is fairly obvious that his own prophecy was the book in question.

Daniel and the Second Coming

The book of Daniel is in a class of its own. It speaks more plainly about Christ's coming to reign over the world than any other Old Testament book. Take this passage, for instance:

> "Behold, with the clouds of heaven there came one like a son of man . . . And to him was given dominion and glory and kingdom, that all peoples, nations, and languages should serve him; his dominion is an everlasting dominion, which shall not pass away, and his kingdom one that shall not be destroyed." (Dan. 7:13, 14.)

Plain enough, isn't it? You would hardly think that anybody could misunderstand words like that.

Yet for a very long time people did misunderstand them. The very early Christians understood them well enough. The writings they left behind show that they believed most fervently in the future kingdom of Christ on earth.

But during the Middle Ages nearly everybody thought that these words of Daniel applied to the Roman Catholic Church! For several centuries prior to the Reformation Daniel's book was, as he had predicted, "shut up" and "sealed".

In those days the great Christian doctrine, that Christ is coming again to rule over the world, was forgotten. So were several other great teachings of the Bible.

At the Reformation the situation improved enormously. Bibles were circulated in great numbers, and greedily read. Many of the "forgotten teachings"—such as justification by faith—were rediscovered.

But some were discovered only by a minority. Even after the Reformation, most of those who repeated the Lord's prayer still did not understand what "Thy kingdom come" meant.

Today, however, the winds of change are blowing again, throughout the whole Christian world. Despite the pathetic way in which leading scholars have tried to undermine men's faith in the Bible, considerable numbers of ordinary men and women are moving closer and closer to God's Word.

All over the world—especially in America and Russia—a steady stream of people are coming to believe that the Lord Jesus will soon return to earth to set up His kingdom. There are still only a relatively small number of them. But the encouraging fact is that their numbers, in this ungodly age, appear to be growing.

To them, the Book of Daniel and the other prophetic Scriptures are no longer "shut up". They "run to and fro" to seek the Word of the Lord, and as their reward their "knowledge is increased".

In this way Daniel's prophecy about his own book is now beginning to be fulfilled, as we enter into "the time of the end". As time goes by the world will sink ever deeper into its final agony. As it does so, increasing numbers of men and women will be driven to turn again to God and His Word. They will seek and they will find, just as Daniel said they would.

It is vitally important that they should "find", just as it is for you and me. For Jesus said:

> "He that believeth and is baptized shall be saved; but he that believeth not shall be damned." (Mark 16:16, AV.)

7

MAN'S FINAL FLING

Thousands of books and pamphlets about the Second Coming have been published. Hundreds of authors have set down their ideas about the sequence of events leading up to Christ's appearance. Unfortunately, no two of them seem to be in complete agreement with each other.

I don't want to add to this confusion by listing all the things that I think might be about to happen. It is better to face up to the truth: the Bible simply does not give enough information to enable us to fill in all the details. And even if it did, we undoubtedly would not be wise enough to understand it all.

Nevertheless, some of the major issues are clear enough. We can be practically certain, for instance, of two things:

(1) In the lead-up to the Second Coming, nations will fight each other in the most appalling war of all time.

(2) At a later stage of events the nations will band together and fight against Christ, who will have to subdue their armies before he can take over the rulership of the world Himself.

Various prophets give us snatches of information about the last great world war. They tell us enough to whet our appetite, but, tantalisingly, not enough to let us identify the main participants for certain.

Daniel describes the last great human conflict as featuring a "king of the north" and a "king of the south". (11:40.) Ezekiel names a whole string of contestants: Gog, Magog, Meshech, Tubal, Gomer, Togarmah, Sheba, Dedan, Tarshish, and several others. (38:1–13.)

The Book of Revelation uses symbols—rather like the subjects of a parable—to refer to the powers involved in Armageddon. There is a "beast", a "false prophet", a "dragon", some "kings from the east", and "three foul spirits like frogs".

Without any doubt, every one of these names and symbols has a latter-day meaning. Within a few years those meanings may become unmistakably plain. In the meantime, suggestions and counter-suggestions abound.

"Gog, Meshech and Tubal" might refer to Russia. So might "the king of the north". There is quite a lot of evidence for this, but not enough to put the matter beyond dispute.

The "king of the south" has been identified with all manner of powers: Egypt, NATO, the black African states, an Arab confederation, and others besides.

Some expositors think the "kings of the east" refers to a group of east Asian powers, dominated by China. Others have applied this to the Arabs, or the Jews, or even to Christ and His disciples.

When the time comes, God will see to it that His people understand these prophecies fully. In the meantime we must be content to "see through a glass, darkly". (1 Cor. 13:12, AV.)

After all, even the twelve apostles did not understand the many Old Testament prophecies about the death and resurrection of Jesus. Those prophecies seem plain enough to us today. but the early disciples, even though they had the Lord Himself as a teacher, could not make sense of those Messianic prophecies until after they were fulfilled.

Even then, it took the resurrected Jesus to open their eyes. He taught them the real meaning of those prophecies about Himself, and they thrilled at the experience. "Did not our hearts burn within us . . . while he opened to us the scriptures?" they said. (Luke 24:32.)

Apparently we need not be ashamed because we don't fully understand all the prophetic Scriptures just yet!

Another example was found in the previous chapter. Some of the prophecies about the Second Coming baffled Bible students for centuries. Then, when the atom bomb was invented, they became full of grim meaning.

In much the same way, the prophecies about the line-up for Armageddon will surely become clear to us as history unfolds.

When Man Fights God

But though we may not know just who fights whom in the early stages of Armageddon, there is no such difficulty about its climax.

At the end, the nations of the whole world will be on the same side. They will be united against a common foe. *Their enemy will be God and the Lord Jesus Christ.*

David wrote a Psalm about this great struggle.

> "The kings of the earth set themselves, and the rulers take counsel together, against the Lord and his anointed, saying, 'Let us burst their bonds asunder, and cast their cords from us.'
>
> "He who sits in the heavens laughs; the Lord has them in derision. Then he will speak to them in his wrath, and terrify them in his fury, saying, 'I have set my king on Zion, my holy hill . . . You are my son, today I have begotten you. Ask of me, and I will make the nations your heritage, and the ends of the earth your possession. You shall break them with a rod of iron, and dash them in pieces like a potter's vessel.' " (Ps. 2:2–9.)

This is another of those prophecies that have a double application. We know that it had a partial fulfilment in the first century. This happened when the Jewish king, Herod, and the Roman governor, Pontius Pilate, sided together in sending Jesus to the cross. The New Testament tells us so. (Acts 4:25–27.)

But this cannot have been the complete meaning of David's prophecy. Some parts of it were never fulfilled. Christ has not yet received the ends of the earth as a possession. Still less has He dashed the rebellious nations in pieces as a potter's vessel.

Evidently history is going to repeat itself—but with a different sequel. When Jesus stood before Pilate, the leaders of the Jews demanded, "Crucify him! . . . We have no king but Caesar." (John 19:15.) Their cruel request was granted.

Human nature has not changed. When the Lord Jesus comes again most of mankind is sure to reject Him once more. But this time the Lord's enemies will not get their own way. They will be destroyed by Christ's supernatural power as the terrible, final fulfilment of David's prophetic psalm takes place.

Another prophecy of this event is found in the Book of Revelation:

> "The ten horns that you saw are ten kings who have not yet received royal power, but they are to receive authority as kings for one hour, together with the beast. These are of one mind, and give over their power and authority to the beast; they will make war on the Lamb, and the Lamb will conquer them . . ." (Rev. 17:12–14.)

God's Last Great Enemy

What is this beast that leads the last fight of mankind against God?

To answer this question we need to go back to the prophecy of Daniel. Like so much else in the Book of Revelation, the beast has its origins in this Old Testament book.

In chapter 7 Daniel described a strange vision. He saw a procession of beasts emerging from the sea.

God told the prophet that this vision was a kind of parable of human history. The four beasts represented four great empires that would pass across the stage of history.

In chapter 2, Daniel gives us another parable of the same period of history, and in chapter 8 a parable of a portion of it. These other chapters are valuable because they actually name the first three great empires.

The first was the Babylonian Empire. (Dan. 2:37, 38.)

The second was the empire of the Medes and Persians. (Dan. 8:20.)

The third was the Greek Empire. (Dan. 8:21.)

The fourth empire was not named. But the fourth beast was described as great, and strong, and terrible. And the Greek Empire was in fact followed by just such an empire—the great, and strong, and terrible empire of Rome.

These were not just local empires. Each of them in turn ruled over all the countries that mattered, as seen from the point of view of a dweller in Bible lands. In Daniel's phrase, these emperors ruled "over all the earth". (Dan. 2:39; 7:23; 8:5.) From the prophet's standpoint, these were *worldwide* empires.

Daniel was quite emphatic that this fourth all-embracing empire would not be followed by a fifth. It would be broken up into a group of independent kingdoms, represented by ten horns growing out of the head of the fourth beast.

This may seem a peculiar way of prophesying the future course of world history. But the fact remains that Daniel's prophecy has come true. There *were* four great empires, so comprehensive as to be regarded by their inhabitants as worldwide.

Yet there were *only* four. Ever since the break-up of Rome, Europe and Asia have been made up of a considerable number of independent nations—just as Daniel foretold.

These independent nations would occupy the scene, said Daniel, until "one like a son of man" came to rule the world in their place.

But Daniel gave a hint that the nations would momentarily be welded into an enormous empire again, just at the time when the Messiah came to take over the government of the world. The body of the fourth beast—not just the horns but *the whole body*—was to be destroyed to make way for Messiah's kingdom.

A Strange Statue

A similar hint is given in Daniel 2. There the history of the Mediterranean world was depicted in terms of a statue—or image, as Daniel called it—made from a strange assortment of materials. This was another parable of the four great empires, and of the divided world that would follow.

The golden head of the image represented the age of Daniel and Nebuchadnezzar, in the sixth century B.C. Its silver chest, its bronze tummy and its iron legs were the Medo-Persian, Greek and Roman empires. Its feet were made of a weird mixture of iron and clay; they represented the hotchpotch of independent nations which were to follow the break-up of Rome.

Our own day corresponds to the tips of the statue's feet. Daniel portrayed Messiah as a stone that would strike the image on its feet and destroy it; this represented the overthrow of all human governments.

It is significant that Messiah was to destroy *the whole statue,* including the parts that represented the worldwide empires of the past, and not just the feet. This suggests that Christ will have to destroy some sort of universal empire when He returns.

Perhaps it will be a revival of the old Roman Empire, occupying much the same territory as before. That would make it a kind of super Common Market, stretching all the way from the Atlantic to the Middle East. Or perhaps (and more probably, in my opinion) it will be something bigger still—a truly worldwide empire.

Four Beasts in One

These hints are supported by the Book of Revelation. There, in chapter 13, Daniel's four beasts reappear. But this time, the four beasts are all rolled into one.

We can see that this is so by analysing Daniel's beasts, and then adding up their parts. This is what we get:

THE FOUR BEASTS OF DANIEL 7

BEAST	NATURE	NO. OF HEADS	NO. OF HORNS
1st	A lion (verse 4)	1	0
2nd	A bear (verse 5)	1	0
3rd	A leopard (verse 6)	4	0
4th	An indescribable monster (verse 7)	1	10
TOTAL	Lion + bear + leopard + monster	7 heads	10 horns

Now compare the results of this addition sum with the beast of Revelation:

"And I saw a beast rising out of the sea (Daniel's beasts, by the way, all came out of the sea) with *ten horns* and *seven heads* . . . And the beast that I saw was like a *leopard*, its feet were like a *bear's*, and its mouth was like a *lion's* mouth. And to it the *dragon* gave his power." (Rev. 13:1, 2.)

The correspondence is striking. Seven heads; ten horns; lion + bear + leopard + monster. This cannot be a coincidence. It must surely be Scripture's way of saying to us, "This beast is Daniel's four beasts compressed into one. It is the greatest, most fearful world-empire of all time."

Further down the chapter this conclusion is confirmed:

> "The beast . . . was allowed to make war on the saints and to conquer them. And authority was given it over every tribe and people and tongue and nation, and all who dwell on earth will worship it, every one whose name has not been written . . . in the book of life." (Rev. 13:5–8.)

The picture is frightening. A fierce political power, ruling over all nations, demanding absolute subjection from everyone, and ruthlessly persecuting those who remain faithful to Christ.

(It must be a political power, and not the Roman Catholic Church as some expositors have suggested. Beasts are never used as symbols of churches in Scripture—not even of churches that have departed from the teaching of the Bible. Scripture uses women to symbolise churches. Wild beasts always represent nations and governments.[1])

There is only one good thing about this fearful beast: its reign of terror is short-lived. It holds sway for only three and a half years. (Rev. 13:5.) Then, in its arrogant madness, it leads the kings of the earth into battle against Christ, who destroys it.

This power that leads man's final fling against God has not yet arisen. When it does there will be no difficulty in recognising it, because nothing quite like it has ever been seen on earth before.

It will be fiercely opposed to everything connected with God. It will demand the abject obedience of all its subjects. Men will be expected to practically worship this ungodly world-state.

It is easy to see how such a power could arise in the earth. The scientific materialism of our age provides the necessary philosophical background for an all-out attack on religion.

The communist countries have shown us what can happen when atheism dominates the government of an individual nation. One can imagine what will happen when an atheist group gains control of the whole world.

When it does happen, God's people will at least be prepared for it.

8

WORLD GOVERNMENT — AT LAST

In Orwell's prophetic novel, *Nineteen Eighty-four*, there was a government department called the Ministry of Peace. Its business was to make war.

But when Jesus rules the earth, He will be a real Minister of Peace. His brief campaign against the beast and his armies really will be a "war to end wars".

The Old Testament gave Him this name: *Prince of Peace.* (Isa. 9:6.) Angels celebrated His birth by singing, "Glory to God in the highest, and *on earth peace among men* . . ." (Luke 2:14.)

God always keeps His promises. But He does so in His own way and in His own time. Jesus has already brought peace to the hearts of His followers. When He comes again He will fill the whole wide world with lasting peace.

In chapter 4 we looked at a number of passages promising this. One of them, which was only quoted in part in that chapter, now deserves a closer look.

> "The wolf shall dwell with the lamb, and the leopard shall lie down with the kid, and the calf and the lion and the fatling together, and a little child shall lead them. The cow and the bear shall feed; their young shall lie down together; and the lion shall eat straw like the ox.
>
> "The sucking child shall play over the hole of the asp, and the weaned child shall put his hand on the adder's den. They shall not hurt or destroy in all my

holy mountain; for the earth shall be full of the knowledge of the LORD as the waters cover the sea." (Isa. 11:6–9.)

Just what does this mean? Are the carnivorous animals really going to become vegetarians?

The lion has claws designed for catching his prey, and teeth made for tearing it apart. His stomach is built to digest raw meat, and cannot cope with grass. Is the lion going to be given a differently shaped mouth in the Kingdom, so that he can crop the grass alongside the sheep? Will God provide him with a set of stomachs like the cow's so that he can assimilate his new diet?

To these questions there is only one safe answer: perhaps. God undoubtedly could change the physical nature of the animals He created if He so wished. Perhaps He will.

But it is equally possible that Isaiah's words are not intended to be taken quite so literally. In the original Hebrew this part of Isaiah is in the form of a poem, and poetry often conveys its message in figurative language.

Perhaps Isaiah really meant that the wild animals will become well-disposed towards man, so that they will no longer be a threat to human life, even though they may remain the same carnivorous beasts that God created.

If this is so, then we have here the solution to yet another world problem. If the wild animals are going to become friends of mankind, the friendship will have to be a two-sided affair. The leopard is no longer a threat to Man, but, as we saw in chapter 1, Man is threatening the very existence of the leopard and lots of other animals.

In God's kingdom this threat will be removed. The wild animals will treat Man well and Man will treat them well. Like many other exploited parts of God's creation, the wild beasts will be restored to their rightful place.

But this does not exhaust the meaning of Isaiah's prophetic words. They almost certainly have a second and deeper meaning.

We have already seen how certain symbolic prophecies use savage beasts to represent ruthless political powers. The symbol is an apt one. When men oppress their fellows they are behaving like beasts.

The Lord Jesus Christ saw the persecution of His disciples in this light. "Behold," He said to them, "I send you out as lambs in the midst of wolves." (Luke 10:3.)

For nineteen centuries there has always been some part of the world where Christ's flock has had to meet in secret for fear of the "wolves". In the Kingdom this will all be changed: the "wolf" then will dwell with the "lamb", and a little child shall lead them.

Other ancient hatreds will be gone, too. Isaiah's poetry makes us think of Africans, Asians and Europeans, of workers and managers, of teenagers and the middle-aged—indeed, of all the groups that now distrust and misunderstand each other—learning to live together in friendly harmony.

In a world that is being torn asunder by narrow self-interest and party strife, well might men plead, "Thy kingdom come".

Solving the World's Food Problem

When you travel the world on Christ's business you rub shoulders with all classes of mankind. Often I have been reminded of Paul's words, "I know how to be abased, and I know how to abound . . . I have learned the secret of facing plenty and hunger, abundance and want." (Phil. 4:12.)

In America I have been plied with rich foods until I have had to cry out to my hosts that they were killing me with their kindness.

In Africa I have given thanks in a mud hut for a meal

of beans and rice which, by local standards, was generous hospitality indeed.

Experiences like this underline the tragedy of our age. Hundreds of millions of us have more to eat than is good for us; hundreds of millions of others are half starved.

Nations like our own give surplus food crops to animals, or keep them until they go bad and then dump them. Meanwhile the population of some countries increases faster than their food production; the number of hungry children in the world gets larger every year.

It seems completely beyond Man's ability to solve the world's food problem. But it will be no problem to the Lord God Almighty. When Christ rules there will be food in abundance for everybody. Here are two of the prophecies that promise us this:

> "The wilderness and the dry land shall be glad, the desert shall rejoice and blossom ... For waters shall break forth in the wilderness, and streams in the desert; the burning sand shall become a pool." (Isa. 35:1–7.)

> "There shall be abundance of corn in the earth upon the top of the mountains; the fruit thereof shall shake like Lebanon." (Ps. 72:16, RV.)

Only during the past few years have men begun to talk about large-scale irrigation of the desert and the use of unproductive land. So far they have not done much about it. Human skill and resources are hopelessly inadequate for such an enormous task.

But God foresaw the need thousands of years before we did. There will be no hunger in Christ's kingdom, thanks to the agricultural revolution that He will supervise.

Divine Physician

As everyone knows, when Jesus was first on the earth He worked miracles. These were intended to show that the power and the love of God were working through Him.

But they also served another purpose. His miracles—and those that He enabled His followers to perform—were an indication of the great things He will do when He comes again. In the words of an apostle, they were a foretaste of the powers of the age to come. (Heb. 6:5.)

Jesus once fed five thousand people with five loaves and two fishes. This was a sign that He was "the Bread of Life", spiritual food for a dying race. But it was more than that. It was also a token that nobody in the world will starve when Jesus rules.

In the same way His miracles of healing were a preview of bigger things to come. There will be no homes for incurables in the coming Kingdom, for:

> "Then the eyes of the blind shall be opened, and the ears of the deaf unstopped; then shall the lame man leap like a hart, and the tongue of the dumb sing for joy." (Isa. 35:5, 6.)

Although our doctors can cure a lot of things, there is one complaint that beats them every time: old age. Over three thousand years ago, the span of Man's life was threescore years and ten. (Ps. 90:10.) It is still much the same today.

When the divine physician is back on earth there will be a startling change. Men will not only be healthier, they will live longer, too:

> "No more shall there be in it an infant that lives but a few days, or an old man who does not fill out his days, for the child shall die a hundred years old, and the sinner a hundred years old shall be accursed.

> "They shall build houses and inhabit them; they shall plant vineyards and eat their fruit. They shall not build and another inhabit; they shall not plant and another eat; for like the days of a tree shall the days of my people be, and my chosen shall long enjoy the work of their hands." (Isa. 65:20–22.)

There will be a good reason for the remarkable health men will enjoy in the kingdom of God. They will get what they will deserve. Their bodily health will reflect their spiritual health.

In other words, the whole population of the world will at long last discover the right way to live. After learning that selfishness leads to disaster, the inhabitants of the Kingdom will find that loving service to God is a much better way of life.

One result of this will be that everybody will be treated fairly. As the words quoted above from Isaiah indicate, men will not be allowed to exploit their fellows.

In the Kingdom there will be no homeless workmen labouring to build houses for other men to live in, or half-starved peasants working on the land while wealthy land-owners reap the rewards. Instead, says Isaiah, the people in God's kingdom "shall long enjoy the work of their hands".

Every form of human wickedness will be thoroughly suppressed. In the figurative language of the Book of Revelation, Satan will be bound with a chain and sealed up. (20:1–3.)

Prophet after prophet depicts the nations of the world learning to serve the Lord and worship Him. Here are two examples:

> "From new moon to new moon, and from sabbath to sabbath, all flesh shall come to worship before me, says the LORD." (Isa. 66:23.)

"Then will I turn to the peoples a pure language, that they may all call upon the name of the LORD, to serve him with one consent." (Zeph. 3:9, AV.)

Thus even the world's great language problem will be solved in the Kingdom. Mankind will at last have a universal tongue. This will doubtless help international relations. But that will not be its main purpose, according to Zephaniah.

Men will use their universal language for the highest of all purposes—to praise the Lord with one accord.

In this way there will not only be peace on earth.

There will also be glory to God in the highest.

Reigning With Christ

Putting the world right will be a tremendous job—even for the all-powerful Son of God. He does not propose to tackle it on His own. He intends to enlist the aid of the immortals for this task.

Jesus made this clear in an answer to a very important question. "Lo, we have left everything and followed you," said Peter. "What then shall we have?"

Jesus replied: "In the new world, when the Son of man shall sit on his glorious throne, you who have followed me will also sit on twelve thrones, judging the twelve tribes of Israel." (Matt. 19:27, 28.)

The picture is breathtaking. In the coming Kingdom—"the new world" as Jesus called it in this verse—there will be a vast population of ordinary, mortal, flesh-and-blood people on the earth. They will be the survivors of the War of Armageddon and their descendants, and will include the twelve tribes of Israel.

These people will need wise and faithful rulers. The immortal followers of Christ, their newly resurrected bodies shining with the glory of God, will supply that need.

What better way could there be of spending a portion of eternity? To help other men and women tread the uphill road to immortality, after we ourselves have been gifted with it—why, that will be joyful service indeed!

This is not just a job for the twelve apostles to do. It is something that the humblest disciple can aspire to. Scripture repeatedly tells us this:

> "If we have died with him, we shall also live with him; if we endure *we shall also reign with him.*" (2 Tim. 2:11, 12.)

> "Thou wast slain and by thy blood didst ransom men for God from every tribe and tongue and people and nation, and hast made them a kingdom and priests to our God, and *they shall reign on earth.*" (Rev. 5:9, 10.)

> "Blessed and holy is he who shares in the first resurrection! Over such the second death has no power, but they shall be priests of God and of Christ and *they shall reign with him a thousand years.*"(Rev. 20:6.)

Here is the perfect answer to the unbeliever's scornful complaint, that eternal life would only be a bore. God does not intend the immortals to have an eternal holiday; He has plenty of satisfying work for them to do.

We may not know all that the future holds in store for the Lord's redeemed. But one thing, at least, has been revealed to us.

For the first thousand years after Christ returns His immortal followers will be kept busy, as they help Him to set the world right and keep it right.

Perfection at Last

Delightful though it may be, the reign of Christ and His immortals on earth will only be a temporary phase. It is bound to be, because the flesh-and-blood subjects of the Kingdom will still be imperfect. And God will not tolerate imperfection for ever.

The subjects of Christ's kingdom will live happier, cleaner, better lives than any generation before them. Yet they will still be mortal men and women, sinners in need of redemption.

So God has set a time limit on this period: "They shall reign with him a thousand years."[1] (Rev. 20:6.)

By the end of that millennium the mortal population of the world will probably be enormous. The increase in the human life-span foretold by Isaiah will probably lead to an even faster population increase than the one we are facing at present.

But it will not be a runaway population explosion like ours today. It will be a planned expansion, carefully controlled by an all-wise King. As we have seen, the deserts and the mountains are going to be cultivated. When that happens the world will be able to support many times its present population.

After a thousand years like this, enormous numbers of mortals will have shown themselves fit to enter eternity. Once more it will be time for a change.

So Christ will again separate the faithful from the unfaithful, just as He will have done at His second coming. Once more He will give immortality to those who are fit for such a wonderful gift, and eternal destruction to the rest.

Then—what next? Let the apostle Paul take up the tale:

> "Then cometh the end, when he (Jesus) shall deliver up the kingdom to God, even the Father; when he shall have abolished all rule and all authority and power. For he must reign, till he hath put all his enemies under his feet.

"The last enemy that shall be abolished is death . . . And when all things have been subjected unto him, then shall the Son also himself be subjected to him that did subject all things unto him, *that God may be all in all*." (1 Cor. 15:24–28, RV.)

God all in all. Just four short words. Yet never did eleven letters speak of greater things.

God all in all. A whole universe rejoicing in the presence of its Creator. No sin, no death, not a blemish remaining. God Himself filling the consciousness of every living spirit—and a myriad immortal sons of God that are glad to have it so.

But this, perhaps, is going a little too far and too fast. Scripture tells us next to nothing about what will happen after the millennium. It may not be wise to dwell too much upon the little it does say.

After all, a thousand years will be quite long enough to learn all about the final stages of God's eternal purpose. At present we can be better occupied yearning for the next step, and praying:

"Thy kingdom come."

9

STEPS TO TAKE

From time to time various well-meaning folk have laid down the law on how to prepare for the Second Coming. In extreme cases their prescription has run something like this:

"First, decide on the exact date when you are expecting the Lord. A few days beforehand, sell up your home and throw in your job. You'll not be needing them any more.

"When the great day draws near, climb a mountain. (If possible do it at night—it's more romantic that way.) Once arrived at the summit, rid yourself of your last earthly possession—your clothes. Then go down on your knees and wait."

Jesus was careful to discourage this sort of foolishness. There was to be no excited preparation for some particular date because "you know neither the day nor the hour." (Matt. 25:13.)

Instead, the Christian was to spend his whole life in a permanent state of readiness. As Jesus said in another chapter:

> "Watch therefore, for you do not know on what day your Lord is coming. But know this, that if the householder had known in what part of the night the thief was coming, he would have watched and would not have let his house be broken into. Therefore you also must be ready; for the Son of man is coming at an hour you do not expect." (Matt. 24:42–44.)

What does this mean in practice? How does the Christian obey His Lord's command to watch for His return?

Obviously we are not intended to live with our heads in the clouds, so obsessed with the idea of Christ's coming that we are oblivious to the world around us.

Nor does God want us to go to the other extreme and keep our eyes fixed on the ground. The world is in a terrible plight which we dare not ignore. But we must not for a moment imagine that we can put the world right ourselves. That is what Christ is coming back to do.

Nevertheless there are things we can do to make our own little corner of the world a slightly better place, and it is a Christian duty to do them.

As we saw in chapter 3, God commanded Israel to respect Nature and live in harmony with it. By disregarding this commandment the world is bringing disaster upon itself. By showing your own respect for Nature you can achieve two valuable results.

First, your own life will become more satisfying and healthier. Secondly, you will be making a useful testimony to the unbelievers around you, by showing that God's Word is very relevant to the problems of the world in which we live.

Respecting Nature

For a simple example, take the question of litter. Have you ever stepped eagerly into the sea, expecting a delicious swim, only to cut your foot on a broken beer bottle or an old tin can?

If so, you will hardly need telling that it is a Christian duty not to spoil the environment by leaving rubbish around. Other people's litter gives you displeasure. Consequently Christ's golden rule, "As you wish that men would do to you, do so to them", insists that you should do your bit to keep the world clean and tidy.

A more subtle offence against Nature is the indiscriminate use of insecticides.

I was once in a friend's house when a solitary fly appeared. It was a lazy slow-moving insect, and he could easily have swatted it with a rolled-up newspaper as his grandfather would have done. But my friend was far too up-to-date for such methods.

He dashed for his aerosol spray and pursued the offending insect around the room in a cloud of foul-smelling chemical fog. In the end the fly gave up the unequal struggle, but by this time the room was hardly fit for human habitation.

Like many people my friend seemed blissfully unaware that insecticides are poisons. Scientists trying to find out if they are harmful to man have sometimes made themselves ill, merely by spreading small quantities on their skins.

Insecticides can be put in the same broad category as X-rays, sleeping tablets, pain killers, and a hundred and one other products of our technological age. For use with discretion, on the rather rare occasions when they are really needed, they can be very valuable. Used to excess they can do more harm than good.

Before you get out the garden sprayer and start dealing out liquid death with careless abandon, pause for a moment and consider the debit side of such chemicals.

If you are old enough to do so, cast your mind back to the days when hosts of coloured butterflies gave added interest and beauty to our gardens. Alas, they succumbed to DDT far more readily than the greenfly at which we aimed it.

Before you press the spray-gun trigger, remember that many of the bodies of the insects you poison will be eaten by song birds. There are several reasons for the decline in the songbird population of our country, one of which is insecticide poisoning. Every can of insecticide used without good reason is another nail in our feathered friends' coffin.

This is not the sentimental plea of a few cranks. Biologists and naturalists the world over are now making the same appeal: only spray when you really have to.

Poison: For Internal Use Only

American writer Mark Waters was very, very ill. He knew that he had only a few days to live. Bracing himself, he started to write his last newspaper article.

His story was not pleasant to write, even though it was all about himself. It began with the day, forty-two years before, when he started smoking at the age of fourteen. It ended with a description of his sufferings over the past few years, since he went down with the lung cancer that killed him.

"Whether this story will stop anyone from smoking, I don't know," he concluded. "I doubt it. Not a soul I've preached to has quit smoking—not a single, solitary soul.

"You always think: 'It will happen to the other guy; never to me.'

"But when you get your lung cancer—God help you."

Waters had learnt, when it was too late, that you can't go on sucking poisons into the human body indefinitely without Nature kicking back.

According to the American Public Health Service the average heavy smoker is cutting eight years off his life. Eight years!

If someone put a medicine on sale that would add eight years to a man's life, people would gladly sell up their homes in order to buy it. Yet the smoker can get this tremendous blessing just by giving up his cigarettes[1]—and actually put money into his pocket as a side benefit.

Now that the evil effects of tobacco smoke on the

human body are established beyond doubt, every smoking Christian needs to reconsider the advice of Paul: "So, whether you eat or drink, or whatever you do, do all to the glory of God." (1 Cor. 10:31.)

Poisons even worse than tobacco are steadily increasing their popularity. While the average British non-smoker does not die until he is in his seventies, and the average cigarette smoker in his sixties, the typical heroin addict dies while still *in his thirties.* If you are ever tempted to experiment—just once—with drugs, remember what the Bible warns about another form of skating on thin ice: "Can a man carry fire in his bosom, and his clothes not be burned?"(Prov. 6:27.)

Those of us who neither smoke nor take drugs need to watch out. There was once a man, said the Lord Jesus, who tried to take a splinter out of another man's eye when he had a whole great plank sticking out of his own eye . . .

Looking After Your Body

"I've just had a remarkable experience," a colleague said to me one day. "I went to a meal with a whole crowd from the . . . church." (He named a community that are famous for their rejection of everything they regard as "worldly".)

"My, can't they eat! I've never seen anything like it. It seems as if, having given up every other sin, they simply have to let themselves go when they get to the table."

It is worth remembering that there is such a sin as gluttony, and that the Bible warns us against it: "Be not among winebibbers, or among gluttonous eaters of meat; for the drunkard and the glutton will come to poverty." (Prov. 23:20, 21.)

This tells us that gluttony and alcoholism are sins bringing their own natural punishment. In extreme cases they can lead men to poverty and ruin their lives. Even the milder forms of over-indulgence in food or drink can do us more harm than we might think.

Despite this, there is no call for a Christian to become a dietetic crank. Taken to extremes, faddiness about food can become almost a rival religion.

And yet the fact remains that a Christian's stomach is not his own; it belongs like the rest of his body to God. It is well worth while to stick to a sensible balanced diet, avoiding any excess of rich foods and drinks. By treating our bodies kindly we are bound to get that little bit of extra strength which we can devote to the joyful service of our Lord.

Similarly we must recognise that our bodies need exercise. God made them that way. One of the evil features of our civilisation is the way it encourages us to avoid exerting ourselves.

If you are an office worker, face up to this fact: you are condemned to a most unnatural way of life. This makes it essential to seize every opportunity for exercise that comes your way.

Try not to use lifts (unless you happen to work at the top of the Empire State Building.) Walking up stairs is marvellously good for you. Running up two at a time is even better, if you are young enough.

Don't get the car out or hop on a bus if you have only a short journey to make. Walk! If everybody followed your example our cities would have less traffic congestion, cleaner air, and smaller queues at the doctors' surgeries.

Ignoring the Joneses

A healthy mind is even more important than a healthy body. Unfortunately it is very difficult to preserve a healthy mind in a world like ours.

We saw in an earlier chapter how the root cause of our planet's mounting crisis is human greed, or covetousness as the Bible usually calls it.

Our whole economic system runs on covetousness. The supply of cheap goods depends upon a continually expanding market. To make the market grow, a vast advertising industry plays upon our natural desires, making us want things we don't really need.

By supplying those unnecessary things at an ever increasing rate our industries are plundering the world of its resources and filling it with junk. Even more serious, they are filling our minds with a wrong attitude to material things.

Steadily increasing prosperity doesn't bring happiness. We only think it does. But because we are always pursuing happiness and never capturing it, ours is a disappointed, discontented age. More than ever before, we need the Bible's warnings about materialism:

> "Take heed (said Jesus) and beware of all covetousness; for a man's life does not consist in the abundance of his possessions." (Luke 12:15.)

> "There is great gain (said Paul) in godliness with contentment; for we brought nothing into the world, and we cannot take anything out of the world; but if we have food and clothing, with these we shall be content." (1 Tim. 6:6–8.)

Contentment. It's a beautiful word. Say it out loud, and savour its gentle soft-sounding syllables.

Contentment, the basis of lasting happiness. It is such a precious thing, and yet so lightly esteemed in these hectic nineteen-seventies.

Our Lord foresaw that it would be. In His great prophecy about the last days He ended with a warning especially for the people of our age:

> "Take heed to yourselves lest your hearts be weighed

down with dissipation and drunkenness and cares of this life, and that day (of His second coming) come upon you suddenly like a snare; for it will come upon all who dwell upon the face of the whole earth.

"But watch at all times, praying that you may have strength to escape all these things that will take place, and to stand before the Son of Man." (Luke 21:34–36.)

A careful look at these words of Christ reveals that He foresaw "dissipation, drunkenness and the cares of this life" as the besetting sins of our age.

They are the "things that will take place" in the last days, Jesus indicates. And He specially advises our generation to pray that we "may have strength to escape all these things . . . and to stand before the Son of man."

So there are at least two good reasons for opting out of the rat race and seeking contentment.

The first is that this is the way to mental health and happiness.

The second is an even better reason. It is also the way to eternal life.

So forget about the Joneses. If they go on as they are doing, Jesus says they will be caught like animals in a snare when He comes again. They are on their way to perdition. Who wants to keep up with folk like that?

Jesus tells us of a better goal to aim at:

> "Take no thought, saying, 'What shall we eat?' or, 'What shall we drink?' or, 'Wherewithal shall we be clothed?' (For after all these things do the Gentiles seek.)
>
> "For your heavenly Father knoweth that ye have need of all these things. *But seek ye first the kingdom of God and his righteousness*; and all these things shall be added unto you." (Matt. 6:31–33, AV.)

Shining Lights

Historians are impressed by the general similarity between our age and the days of ancient Rome.

At its first-century peak the Roman civilisation was remarkably advanced. Rome's engineers had developed technologies that put them far ahead of the rest of the world. In consequence the citizens of Rome were exceedingly prosperous.

As with us, their prosperity brought a pollution problem. All round the edge of the city were huge refuse pits. Sewage, rotten food, and even human carcases were dumped in these foul holes.

When the archaeologist Rodolfo Lanciani opened up one of these pits he had an unpleasant surprise. "The stench from that putrid mound, turned up after a lapse of twenty centuries, was unbearable," he wrote.[2] The Romans must have paid a high price in ill-health for their unhygienic habits—just as we do for ours.

This rich civilisation of Rome was extremely decadent. Roman morals were even worse than those of our own age—although at the present rate of downhill progress it won't be many years before we equal them.

One final point of comparison: mighty, prosperous, corrupt Rome was headed for a national disaster that would lead to Rome's utter ruin.

In this world which was so like ours the early Christians lived. To the church in the Roman city of Philippi, Paul gave some advice that is equally appropriate to us:

> "Be blameless and harmless, children of God without blemish in the midst of a crooked and perverse generation, *among whom ye are seen as lights in the world*, holding forth the word of life." (Phil. 2:15, 16, RV.)

The world in which they lived was a murky place. It was possible for them to stand out like beacon lights in the darkness. By their godly example they were a standing invitation to others to come and join them. So Paul praised them for "holding forth the word of life".

Just like them the believers of today have a great work to do. We ought never to grumble at the way the world is growing worse and worse. Jesus tells us to look up and lift up our heads as the final chaos approaches, because we know that our own deliverance is drawing close. (Luke 21:28.)

And besides, the more the surrounding darkness deepens, the more effectively your own lamps will be seen to shine. The closer the end approaches the more incentive we shall have to dedicate our lives to the Master's service. As the apostle Peter puts it:

> "What sort of persons ought you to be in lives of holiness and godliness, waiting for and hastening the coming of the day of God, because of which the heavens will be kindled and dissolved, and the elements will melt with fire!" (2 Pet. 3:11, 12.)

There has never been any excuse for a Christian to lack enthusiasm. A few minutes' quiet thought about the Cross of Christ should be enough at any time to set our hearts on fire for Him.

But our poor human nature is weak. The Cross *should* be all we need, but all too often it is not.

We can be thankful that God has given us an additional spur in these last days. The world is careering madly down towards disaster. Every thinking man is aware of that.

The world's leaders are looking frantically for a solution to the world's problems. Some of them are already despondent about the prospect of finding one.

Those who believe the Bible can point to the solution. It is not just a piece of wishful thinking like the so-called solutions of the politicians.

It is a solution that cannot fail, guaranteed by the Word of the Almighty, and backed by two thousand years of prophecies that have already been fulfilled.

This is a tremendous message to offer to a frightened world. It is a message of impending doom for those who are determined to reject God, but of glorious saving hope for those who will believe it.

This is something worth getting excited about. If you believe the Bible, you have something wonderful to tell the world.

Don't keep it back, begs Jesus.

> "You are the light of the world. A city set on a hill cannot be hid. Nor do men light a lamp and put it under a bushel, but on a stand, and it gives light to all in the house.
>
> "Let your light so shine before men, that they may see your good works and give glory to your Father who is in heaven." (Matt. 5:14–16.)

Accepting Jesus

When Jesus preached the Sermon on the Mount He addressed a large crowd of people. Some of them were disciples, others were not. But Jesus gave them the benefit of the doubt. Throughout most of His speech He spoke as if all His hearers were true believers.

At the very end He changed His approach. Lest there should be any misunderstanding He concluded with a warning:

> "Not every one who says to me, 'Lord, Lord', shall enter the kingdom of heaven,[3] but he who does the will of my Father who is in heaven. On that day many will say to me, 'Lord, Lord, did we not prophesy in your name . . . and do many mighty works in your name?'

"And then will I declare to them, 'I never knew you; depart from me, you evildoers.' " (Matt. 7:21–23.)

In this book I have tried to follow the same plan. Generally I have addressed my readers as if they were all disciples of Jesus. Now it is time to recognise that many of them are not disciples—yet.

Perhaps some of them have been impressed with the message of this book. If so, they will not feel happy about their position. They will not relish the prospect of being greeted by Jesus when He returns with the words quoted above: "I never knew you."

If *you* are in this position, let me offer a word of caution. Don't take refuge in the thought, "Perhaps I'm really one of Christ's disciples after all."

Those searching words of Jesus show that it is not enough to be merely a nominal Christian. All the people that Christ said He would reject *thought* they were followers of His. *They* knew *Him*. But He still said, "I never knew you."

Four Vital Needs

The New Testament tells us all the characteristics of a true Christian. There are many of these but four of them stand out above all the rest: faith, faithfulness, prayerfulness and Bible-mindedness.

Faith is the bedrock of Christianity. This is why we speak of "The Christian faith". Without faith we are like a car with a flat battery—we cannot get anywhere. As the apostle said, "Without faith it is impossible to please him (God)." (Heb. 11:6.)

A knowledge of Bible teaching and the way prophecy has been fulfilled can give you grounds for faith.

But they cannot give you faith itself. Only God can do that. And He will give it you, if you ask Him. Jesus promises you that. (Matt. 7:7–11.)

The second great mark of a Christian is what I have called faithfulness. This is not a New Testament word, although the Old Testament often uses it to denote the goodness of God.

It is a useful word, because its meaning embraces those of several New Testament words: love, obedience, works, and others.

It is a good word because it starts with "faith"—and a Christian's "faithfulness" springs out of his faith. "Faith working through love" Paul calls it. (Gal. 5:6.) "I by my works will show you my faith," says James (2:18).

The third outstanding sign of a Christian is prayerfulness. This word is not found anywhere in the Bible, but you cannot read the Bible without realising its importance.

Jesus teaches us to regard God as a loving Father, and to talk to Him as if we were His children.

"Men ought always to pray, and not to faint," He said. (Luke 18:1, AV.) "Pray constantly", advises Paul. (1 Thess. 5:17.)

The word I like to use to describe the other great characteristic of a Christian is Bible-mindedness.

This also is not a Bible word, but the idea behind it is Biblical enough. Isaiah explains it well:

> "This is the man to whom I (God) will look, he that is humble and contrite in spirit, and trembles at my word." (Isa. 66:2.)

Bible-minded men and women know they need the wisdom and the strength that the Bible can give. They use God's Word as the powerhouse of their inner life, as Paul said we ought:

> "All scripture is inspired by God and profitable for teaching, for reproof, for correction, and for training in

righteousness, that the man of God may be complete, *equipped for every good work.*" (2 Tim. 3:16, 17.)

The Bible-minded man doesn't just keep quoting a few favourite verses. He makes himself familiar with every book of the Bible and tries to read a chapter or two every day.

He lets the Bible convey its own message to him, and where the Bible leads, he follows. When the Bible commands, he obeys.

All through his life he turns to the Bible for instruction. Like Saul on the road to Damascus he repeatedly asks, "What shall I do, Lord?" (Acts 22:10.) Again and again the Bible answers him, and he respects the Bible's answer.

When he is fully converted, he humbly obeys the command that was given to the newly converted Saul: "Why do you wait? Rise and be baptised, and wash away your sins, calling on his name." (Acts 22:16.)

The Only Hope

There is only one hope for Planet Earth: the personal return of our Lord and Saviour Jesus Christ.

But this is no message of comfort to those who reject Him. There is only one hope for you: total surrender to the Lord Jesus—now. The books of the Bible will lead you to Him:

> "When you walk, they will lead you; when you lie down, they will watch over you; and when you awake, they will talk with you. For the commandment is a lamp and the teaching a light, and the reproofs of discipline are the way of life." (Prov. 6:22, 23.)

EPILOGUE

Spaceship Earth continues its endless journey around the sun.

The date is a few years away in the future. It is time for another imaginary visit of inspection.

From afar it appears exactly the same shining sphere as ever. But drawing closer it is evident that great changes have taken place. Somehow it looks a cleaner and a healthier ship, even when viewed across a thousand miles of space.

Close up, the improvements are striking. The air is sparkling fresh, the water pure and clear. There are no heaps of sordid ugliness: all is neat and purposeful, yet at the same time gracious.

Men, women and children look healthy, well-fed and, above all, happy. Yet even their happiness is different from the happiness that used to be. This is not the short-lived gaiety of a burdened people seeking temporary escape in recreation.

It is rather the deep, satisfying pleasure that comes from fulfilling Man's deepest yearnings. These are men and women who have found the real purpose of life—and their discovery has made them glad.

They know now whither they are journeying. They know the way to work together, in peace and harmony.

They have learnt to love the Lord their God, and their neighbour as themselves. Human life for the first time in history has become full of meaning and of joy.

The spaceship at last is functioning properly. Its favoured crew have found their destiny. At long last they are living and working and loving as they were always meant to do.

Planet Earth has been transformed.

The Captain is on board once more, and all is well.

Notes and References

Prologue

1. It was the late Adlai Stevenson, then United States representative at the United Nations, who originated the notion of "Spaceship Earth". In a speech to UNO's Economic and Social Council at Geneva he said in 1965:

   "We travel together, passengers on a little spaceship, dependent on its vulnerable supplies of air and soil . . . preserved from annihilation only by the care, the work, and I will say, the love we give our fragile craft."

Chapter 1

1. H. Schroader, "Effect of chromium, cadmium and lead on the growth and survival of rats." *J. Nutrition*, 1963, **80**, p. 48.
2. D. Price, "Is man becoming obsolete?" *Public Health Reports*, 1959, **74**, pp. 693–699.

   Other books relevant to this chapter:
3. R. Carson, *Silent Spring*. Hamish Hamilton, London, 1963.
4. W. Marx, *The Frail Ocean*. Ballantine, New York, 1967.
5. A. Hopcraft, *Born to Hunger*. Heinemann, London, 1968.
6. R. and L. Rienow, *Moment in the Sun*. Ballantine, New York, 1971.

Chapter 2

1. R. Dumont and B. Rosier. Methuen Deutsch, London, 1969.
2. M. Allaby. Tom Stacey, London, 1972.
3. W. and P. Paddock. Little Brown, Boston and Toronto, 1964.
4. G. Borgstrom. Collier, New York and London, 1967.
5. E. Goldsmith (Editor). Tom Stacey, London, 1971.
6. J. A. Loraine. Heinemann, London, 1972.
7. G. R. Taylor. Thames and Hudson, London, 1970.
8. B. Commoner. Jonathan Cape, London, 1972.
9. R. F. Dasmann. Penguin-Unesco, London and Paris, 1972.
10. B. Ward and R. Dubos. André Deutsch, London, 1972.
11. Ward and Dubos, chapter 9.
12. P. R. Ehrlich, *The Population Bomb*. Ballantine, London, 1971.
13. "A Blueprint for Survival", issued by a large team of prominent British scientists. *The Ecologist*, **2**, (1), January 1972, pp. 1–43.

14. W. C. Brown, President of Hercules Inc., in a speech to the annual meeting of the American Institute of Chemical Engineers. Reported in *Chemical Engineering Progress*, **68** (4), April 1972, pp. 33–35.
15. "Blueprint for Survival", pp. 33, 37.
16. Results of a Gallup poll, quoted in *The Times*, 15th January 1973.
17. Dr. D. M. Fanning, "Families in Flats". *British Medical Journal*, 1967, pp. 383–6.
18. According to Dr. R. E. Helfer, of the University of Colorado School of Medicine. (Reported.)
19. Martin Secker and Warburg, London, 1969.
20. Lord Ritchie-Calder, *Hell Upon Earth*. The Conservation Society, London, 1968.
21. N. Calder (editor) *Unless Peace Comes*. Allen Lane, London, 1968.
22. R. Clarke, *We All Fall Down—The Prospects of Chemical and Biological Warfare*. Allen Lane, London, 1968.
23. *New Scientist*, 21st September 1972, back cover.
24. Quoted by Prof. Barry Commoner, in *Science and Survival*. Gollancz, London, 1966.
25. *The Glasgow Herald*, 25th November 1969.
26. Dedication of *Silent Spring* (R. Carson. Hamish Hamilton, London, 1963.)

Other books relevant to this chapter:

27. P. R. and A. H. Ehrlich, *Population, Resources, Environment* (2nd edition). W. H. Freeman, San Francisco, 1972.
28. D. H. Meadows and others, *The Limits to Growth*. Universe Books, New York, and Earth Island, London, 1972.

Chapter 3

1. R. Dubos, "A Theology of the Earth". Smithsonian Institution, Washington, 1969.

Chapter 4

1. Bertrand Russell, "Is a Third World War Inevitable?" *World Horizon*, 1950, **1** (2), pp. 6–9.

2, 3. I have used the words of the Authorised Version in these two quotations because they are familiar—thanks to Handel's *Messiah*.

Chapter 6

1. B. Ward and R. Dubos, *Only One Earth* (Penguin, London, 1972), ch. 9, pp. 187 and 189.
2. Religious Tract Society, London, 1887.
3. John Hersey, *Hiroshima* (Penguin, London, 1946), ch. 3, pp. 64–5.
4. ibid., p. 73.

Chapter 7

1. See, for example, 2 Cor. 11:2; Rev. 21:2, 9 (women) and 2 Tim. 4:17; Matt. 10:16 (wild beasts).

Chapter 8

1. Some of the numbers in the Book of Revelation seem to be symbolic numbers, not meant to be taken literally. For example, it is unlikely that the Holy City of Revelation 21:16 will really be more than a thousand miles high! The "thousand years" of the first stage of Christ's kingdom may be a literal 1,000 years. But it is equally possible that it may merely be a symbolic way of saying, "A very long period".

Chapter 9

1. Strictly speaking, it is only the young, heavy smoker who can add eight years on average to his life if he stops smoking. Light smokers, and people who give up smoking in later life, can still lengthen their lives by giving up, but by a smaller amount.
2. Cited by R. F. Dasmann, in *Planet in Peril*. Penguin-Unesco, London and Paris, 1972.
3. Matthew uses the term "Kingdom of heaven" where the other three gospels use "Kingdom of God". Evidently Jesus used both these phrases interchangeably, as names for His coming kingdom on earth. Both phrases spring from Daniel 2:44, where it is called the kingdom of the God of heaven.

Biblical quotations are all taken from the Revised Standard Version, except where otherwise stated.

Also by Alan Hayward

God's Truth

A scientist shows why it makes sense to believe the Bible

Among the topics discussed are:
Fulfilled prophecy—the 'uninventable' character of Christ —evidence for the Resurrection —the more-than-human foresight of the Law of Moses— the harmony of Scripture
The inspiration and infallibility of the Bible—the authorship of the Biblical books—the accuracy of copyists and translators— problems of interpretation
The historical accuracy of the Bible—apparent errors and contradictions—moral problems
The Bible and science—miracles— the flood—creation—evolution— 'prehistoric man'—the problem of suffering
How to begin to study the Bible —the Bible as a power in our lives

Published by Marshall, Morgan & Scott,
116 Baker Street, London W1M 2BB